*

Beauty Eating Beauty

*

Beauty Eating Beauty

Poems

Nancy C. Harris

Portals Press

Cover Art: YAY Images & BW photographs
Cover design: Nancy Harris

Acknowledgments:
Some of the poems in *Beauty Eating Beauty* were first published in *Mirror Wars* (1999, Portals Press). *Mirror Wars* is out of print due to flooding after Hurricane Katrina.
An excerpt of "Beauty Eating Beauty" was printed in the book *Hearing Sappho in New Orleans: The Call of Poetry from Congo Square to the Ninth Ward* (Louisiana State University Press, 2012) by Ruth Salvaggio.
"The Anchoress Reflects on Her Beauty," "Charmed I'm Sure," "Precarious," "Last Bacchanalia on the Carrollton Riviera," and "Hunter's Moon" and "Lotus Eater" first appeared in *Shards*, a chapbook (2002, Umteem Press).
"Still Life w/ Creole Tomatoes" and "Katrina Kristmas" first appeared in the on-line publication, *Big Bridge 16*, ed. Michael Rothenberg and Terri Carrion.
"Katrina Ukhupachacuti" first appeard in the anthology *Continent of Light*, (2011) ed. David Madgalene.
"Momento Mori: The Black Box" was published in the anthologies, *From A Bend in the River, 100 New Orleans Poets*, ed. Kalamu Ya Salaam, and in *Umpteen Ways of Looking at a Possum: Critical and Creative Responses to Everette Maddox*, (2006) ed. Grace Bauer and Julie Kane.
An excerpt of "Memos from the Planchette of HPB" appeared in the *New Orleans Review* special edition, *The Other South*, (1999) ed. Ralph Adamo and Bill Lavender.
"Momento Mori: The Black Box," "Unemployed in Fall #2" and "My Dog Comes to the Word Death" appeared in the anthology *Umpteen Ways of Looking at a Possum: Critical and Creative Responses to Everette Maddox*, ed. Grace Bauer and Julie Kane.
"Beauty Eating Beauty" first appeared in the anthology *The Maple Leaf Rag III*, (2006). "What Bear Wants" and "Bear Market" first appeared in the anthology *The Maple Leaf Rag IV*, (2010).

Beauty Eating Beauty by Nancy Harris
Limited Edition © by Portals Press
New Orleans, Louisiana, USA
www.portalspress.com

© 2013 by Nancy C. Harris
All rights reserved.

ISBN 978-0-916620-13-4

Contents

Beauty Eating Beauty	9
The Anchoress Reflects on Her Beauty	15
KataStrophes	23
Still Life w/Creole Tomatoes	24
Katrina Kristmas	27
Stocking Stuffers—Christmas Day 2006	29
Winter Trees Post-K	31
Winter Trees 2007	32
Attack of the Creole Tomato Cats	33
Katrina Ukhupachacuti	35
All Souls Day / Along the Mississippi	37
Mummings	39
Dutch Boy's Finger	44
Imbolc	46
The Lotus-Eater Gets Her Just Deserts	52
Woman Clothed With the Sun	55
The Wizard Who Fell to Earth as Fellini	59
My Dog Comes to the Word "Death"	62
Memento Mori: The Black Box	64
Rescuing Mr. Redbones	67
Unemployed in Fall	71
Unemployed in Fall #2	73
New Orleans: All Saints Day	75
Precarious	77
Last Bacchanalia at the Carrollton Riviera	80
Charmed, I'm Sure (Celtic Cross)	83
Harvest Moon: Fool in the Pool	91
Hunter's Moon	93
Full Moon in Taurus	95
Memos From the Planchette of HPB	97
Bear Dreams	113
The Care & Feeding of Animal Images	115
What Bear Wants	120

White Spirit Bear Vanishing	123
Bear Floats In My Cerebral Cortex	125
Bear Hibernates En Hiver	126
Bear at the Back Door	128
Bear Comes Home / To Dine On Your Ear	129
Bear Dreams Y2K	130
Bear Market	132
Bear Eats the Mayan Calendar & an Oyster Po-Boy	134
Bear Dreams the Hunter's Moon	137
Bear Dreams Crystal Skulls at the Winter Solstice	139

BEAUTY EATING BEAUTY

> *"The world is charged with the grandeur of God.*
> *It will flame out like shining from shook foil;*
> *It gathers to a greatness, like the ooze of oil*
> *Crushed. Why do men then now not reck his rod?"*
> *– Hopkins, "God's Grandeur"*

1.

Purple orchids punch me in the eye
when I open the back door.
I devour their rudeness – arriving late.
they shouldn't be there in December.
they bruise my retina & astound my sense of purpose.
why am I here? to let out the dogs who bound
oblivious all four of them hell-bent on peeing
while I stand ready to counterattack
reeling in midday sun, blue sky.

2.

Ambushed in October of '01
by the rage of purple and the still-latent
scent of anthrax-laced air
I carried my dying cat Minerva out the back door
onto the deck to hold her for awhile in the sun
the last time she would see or feel its caressing arc
nurturing her diabetic racked frame
fragile and brittle as a bird's nest
a gut-wrenched ending to her tortoise-shell beauty

the orchids stood guard then, too
tensely oblivious
to death & their own beauty
as I pictured tarot trump 16:

Lightning Struck Tower –
only instead of Yods – forked resistance
explosive quincunx

sparking from the building
electric hands of God flaming like *"shook foil"*
I saw TV images of tiny bodies –
far-flung specks hurtling from twin towers:
were they chosen to enter blessed chaos?
total destruction of everything in
the present to make way for what … heads, arms,
torsos, legs, feet all falling
falling away from beauty into flames of resurrection
torched, hacked, gashed, brutal bruises turning purple.

3.

Scarab beetle, cloisonnéd jewel
shimmering green & burgundy
radiant insect—the scientific nomenclature
nature wants eludes me—
has been a rare visitor in my summer yard for decades—
rolling balls of dung to the sun
ancient Egyptian myths unveiled before my eyes –
sitting on my deck I see a large dog turd
heaving up and down
undulating & ugly
what the hell—as I move in closer to investigate
I see the beautiful beetle
underneath like a health-club freak pumping iron
driving the huge dung absurdly careening
a thousand times its weight around the track
bringing shit home to god—
"the achieve of, the mastery of the thing!"

& once at the edge of the pool the scarab
well, not the exact same one, landed where I would rescue
it to the edge to keep the chemicals from
ending its incarnation—I always felt honored when it showed up
a visit from royalty—it appeared dead, morbidly inert
& I said "I love you, please live" —when suddenly it evolved
flew off, phoenix-like. I didn't try to figure it out. It lived
for awhile. my eyes eating beauty, truth, dogshit.

4.

Heavy-weight: lizard vs. dragonfly
see the championship fight at a poetry reading near you.

that spring and summer lizards ruled.
they jumped down from trees into people's hair
usually women's and zigzagged on walls and plants
on the patio of the Maple Leaf Bar.
poets wrote odes to them—one even landed on my head
as I sat under a tree listening to word-molecules
float through the air on a Sunday afternoon.
a visiting poet from Atlanta experimenting in New Orleans,
Lowther by name, happened upon that particular Sunday
to extemporize—not memorize—his poems all in black.
Black eye patches to anaesthetize his senses—synaesthesia—
oblivious to sun shadows trees—sensory deprivation
so the words would come out pure, pristine, elegant
bone-house eating beauty like a huge hunk of Beowulfian bone-grist.
we watched and listened to an unfolding legend—
only spoken not written—but the heat wavered and eyes wandered
& mine fell on the wrought-iron chair before me.
an iridescent blue dragonfly landed on a curve of black iron
and I was mesmerized by its outrageous beauty
showcased in shafts of sunlight—
sequined, glimmering, hovering like a nightclub diva
tunnels of light bathing it with unearthly auras:

the poet in black kept creating wordspells
but the dragonfly kept several of us enthralled;
a perfect moment in time then PLINK
a green lizard plunked down from overhead tree
onto metal chair instantaneously grabbing blue dragonfly
by neck gorging itself munching the exquisite wings
like a diner at a sidewalk café sticking it's fork into
a gourmet caesar salad green leaves sticking out of its craw
savouring each mouthful in oblivious hunger—a true moment
of insidious beauty horrific gluttony—a moment of
gourmand philosophy: beauty eating beauty but who was the chef?

the poet in black embroidered his wordcraft without a clue
to the drama before him. We gasped & tried to grasp the plot.
the lizard preened himself licking its chops heaving a pink pouch
grand with self-esteem gut full.

was the lizard made greater with dragonfly inside
digestive juices eating away at multiplied beauty
or was dragonfly reduced
in the alembic stomach of lizard?
transformation between elements
something new or old?
only overcomplicated humans
could go on so about such a natural occurrence
being consumed by beauty.
I banish such thoughts.
poets eighty-sixed from Plato's Bar & Grill.

5.

A few days later out on the back deck with dogs
I watch Pandora golden retriever pup stalking
& pouncing, grabbing something in her mouth
chomping with gusto, so I interfere —
a limp, moribund lizard
drops onto the deck. I think maybe it will live.
lizards like to resurrect.
when I come home from work
it is dessicated and faded.

at night on the deck outside with dogs
after work late—I have a night job—
I hear rats scampering across the clear roof
I watch rats slithering on back of neighbors shed
into laundry room while dogs growl and howl.
it's a still night and suddenly windchimes tinkle from the fairy realms
perhaps an angel ... but no, the large black rat unencumbers itself
from the vine that has grown around the chimes: *ratangel* I think
amused at the morph. rat/angel beauty eating beauty the chimes
sound the same. I tell the dogs, get over the rats, they're just rats

running around on their rat errands living their rat lives
like Horton Hears a Who.
a beautiful rat in a Hindu temple sniffs incense
and bows to ratgods. God's a rat.
Iraqui's are rats beheading US citizens/
US soldiers are rats sexually humiliating Iraqui prisoners.
beauty eating beauty:
all good rats go to heaven.
green lizard eating blue dragonfly.
rats. rats. rats.

6.

I pull my car up to the Maple Leaf for a reading.
the cat on the sidewalk in front is Mr. Redbones incarnate.
same markings same color, except for eyes. He's come back!
my beautiful orange tabby who died a month ago.
I yell, Mr. Redbones, it's you! The cat is friendly and comes back
to the back patio with the poets, hangs out with us for the reading.
orange tabby with snake-like markings on forehead.

Barry reads his poem about rats —
rats at the Maple Leaf running across his feet during a reading
while he listened to a poet with his eyes closed.
As he reads, the Mr. Redbones-look-alike
preys with war-like maneuvers upon a green lizard.
poet's words diverted by playful tabbycat on the bricked patio.
a stray we think, needing a meal, let him have his way.
but no, he doesn't want to eat the lizard.
It's just play, catch the quarry, no politics involved
just a rat ringing a windchime. The lizard limps off
to lick its wounds. Poems chime in our ears.
Karel wants to interfere, save the lizard,
but I say they don't do that on wildlife shows.
Karel writes a haiku about cats eating lizards.
when she reads it, the cat pays no attention.

I think of Yeats', "The Cat and the Moon"
where "The pure cold light in the sky/

Troubled his animal soul."
The orange tabby's "changing eyes"
replicate the lizard's changing skin
and deceit rules this world we're in.

lizard/dragonfly/scarab/dog/cat/rat/poet:
we are all prisoners of war:
beauty eating beauty:
purple orchid pulverizing my senses.

Truth is: that's all you need to know.

THE ANCHORESS REFLECTS ON HER BEAUTY

The Solar Angel collects himself, scatters not his force, but, in meditation deep, communicates with his reflection.
    —A.A. Bailey, *Rules for Magic*

I stand like an umbrella
inside my altar
the mirrors that surround
feet to head encircling
rain reflections of my beauty
like thousands of glass beads
falling & scattering from my rosary
the wind distributing the petals
of promise four ways.

Through the beads light refracts
the seven faces of itself
each bead a world on this priceless necklace
which enthralls me: I consummate my vows.

No one will see this
but my beauty reaches itself
out like a peacock's winged
eyes. I am an angel of desire
of purity. No one will see in this
vanity. Too bad some would say
to have gained a perfection for no one.

I turn gradually transparent
as Botticelli would have me
my hair glows blue sparks of fire
matching my lazuli veins
that flow under this crystal
skin like rivers leading
to & from my source

while etchings cut
on the surface of my vessel
arouse magic's mouth:
the uroboros enclosing a pentagram
is a seal of pubic glass
that guards me like the lapis
no one sees
no one can touch
& fish with enamel scales
spawn in my blood
play on the rainbow
of piano keys' crystal
clanking harmony.

My breasts are two mandalas
that swirl with optical illusion
no one sees
red, blue, yellow, green
the patterns rush like rivers
into the mirrors that surround
this living sarcophagus
no one can ever bury or possess:
beauty aching within its own arms
caressing itself shimmering forth.

Radiant, seven arrows of light
shoot from me into the mirrors
echoing me numberless
a thousand times to the infinite power:
arms, legs, torsos, heads, eyes
of me, diced starfish limbs
inflorescent, budding into constellations:
I am the center of this radiance
my own mandala, the labyrinth
whose golden thread I hold like reins
knowing blind its secret paths.
I ride a thousand and one horses
charging brigades of myself
into one cell of sound & light

reproducing into an organism
crystal as Bosch's world
that folds in half over itself
the triptych hidden within
the sin, the delight, the punishment
of the world, as man would see it:
three and two, the pentagram of the body
while a triangle and a square of me
fold into a pyramid by whose power
I rise a seven-sided star
to my infinite power.

I sit in this pulsing self-myriad
like a jade Buddha smiling at dragons.

I allow myself these observations
instead of sticking thorns and metal
into this marked flesh.
I stick its beauty in my eyes'
concentrated pupils like suns
to remind that no one will ever
again see it. I am sealed in
this vessel, this urn
of a house with only a skylight
reflected in the mirrors

I tantalize the light
& bow down to it
on my forehead
a yogic seal.

Never again will I go beyond
the limits of this hermitage
speak with lips
to reach another's ears
never to paste myself with salt
onto the collage of another:
I swear I would eat my children;
blood is the pelican's retort.

All this beauty laid at my feet.
I will meditate for the rest
of my body's span
spangle in the same spot
haloing the light's phrenology.
Prophecies of silence will be loud.
like a spectrum I disperse
from a fountain's spray
falling on seeds that elect only me
to guide them upward
unfolding in the light.

I leave myself often.
Here is the map of my rites:

FIRE PATH:

I waver through the skylight
a whirling disk of fire
I represent it in
red, blue, yellow, green
chemically flaming tincture
I enter an alchemist's glass tube
to alloy or allay, steady or excite
reduce, powder, extend or subtilize
what he's working on, then leave
a trail of colored smoke
become Ezekial's wheel
become a ball of fire for a telescope
become a UFO
become a child's nightmare scream
become a burning spiderweb
for a bush, become
the familiar of a shaman
become a pyramid's god ...

EARTH PATH:

Druids worship within
my mound of Venus
lines of hands
a map of blue veins
I am a ball of dung
a scarab rolls to a pharaoh
I unite myself with fire
for Vesuvius' fury
gliding myself over
a whole city
taxiderming it
with a corpse of earth
worms & snakes
ball into me unconscious
of what they symbolize ...

WATER PATH:

I funnel to the earth's center
a journey needing no map.
lizards & centaurs sniff
at my navel while shipwrecks
enter my womb like abortions.
an octopus' eight arms slaver
over my depths like stars' rays.
I am the Anima of a poet
contemplating suicide
wanting to enter me
but not daring. I egg
him on. I am not real.
skulls float on me like buoys
markers of danger
I bring forth life:
pristine Venus steps out of me.
I am the waterfall of a prism
plunging into the sun ...

WIND PATH:

Nebulous puffs
of me like a sprite
I spire into the wings
of the sky
I twist into a unicorn's horn
into a cyclone destroying.
I inspire the ears of trees
who whisper: bonsai.
I sail salt from the sea
to the earth
I move mountains
I move seeds to fertilize
their opposites. I lick
the tongues of fire. I am
a grand mandala of breath ...

I return through my skull's skylight
cranny in my roof, the hearth, altar
lost in the atomic structure of a word,
I swim into the focus of the mirror's eyes.

Daily I produce beauty no one will see.
unguarded I move through these rooms
the breath from a glassblower's lungs
automatic rhythm hymns
these shapes of crystal stacking
themselves around me
this mute fish opaque as a soul
suspended by water, shaped
by glass skin. I sing.

When I water my plants
they give me a mantra.

Daily I produce beauty no one will see
though I have neighbors & can see straight
into the living room across the street.

I will not break this sealed in vow
that treasures itself
sought after as gold
but not as beautiful as my linen skin
stretched taut as Botticelli would have me:
I am what I reflect.
Painted, my cowl thick as maya
I am lost to the world.
I will never leave this shell.

If you would try to drop me
into a jar of water
I would not expand
my paper beauty into a lotus.
you are no magicians
my hinges would not give
my two halves shell-tight
bivalved within myself.
I clamp this hidden mystery
you would have for yourselves.
No I won't come out

like little wooden awkward people
moving diurnally across the cuckoo's house.
I tell my own time.

If this house caught fire
I still would not come out
to proclaim its hour:
I would be the candle's flame
on top of the brass snake
flaming swirling turning
red, blue, yellow, green
like two hands in prayer
I would disintegrate
& essentially send myself
like an arrow useless to gravity
upwards through my skylight
floating like a lotus across a pond

endlessly toward that moving target
red, blue, yellow, green.
then I would begin the centripetal
unshrouding.
I might as well be dead.

Note

The anchoritic life became widespread during the early and high Middle Ages. Examples of the dwellings of anchorites and anchoresses survive. They tended to be a simple cell, built against one of the walls of the local village church. In the Germanic lands from at least the tenth century it was customary for the bishop to say the office of the dead as the anchorite entered her cell, to signify the anchorite's death to the world and rebirth to a spiritual life of solitary communion with God and the angels. Sometimes, if the anchorite was walled up inside the cell, the bishop would put his seal upon the wall to stamp it with his authority.

Hearing Mass and receiving Holy Communion was possible through a small, shuttered window in the common wall facing the sanctuary, called a "hagioscope" or "squint". There was also a small window facing the outside world, through which the inhabitant would receive food and other necessities and, in turn, could provide spiritual advice and counsel to visitors, as the anchorites gained a reputation for wisdom. Anchorites were supposed to remain in their cell in all eventualities. Some were even burned in their cells, which they refused to leave even when pirates or other attackers were looting and burning their towns.

kata-strophes

catastrophe (kəˈtæstrəfi)
a final decisive event, usually causing a disastrous end

Also called: **cataclysm** any sudden and violent change in the earth's surface caused by flooding, earthquake, or some other rapid process

strophe

c.1600, from Gk. strophe "stanza," originally "a turning," in reference to the section of an ode sung by the chorus while turning in one direction, from strephein "to turn," from PIE *strebh- "to wind, turn" (cf. Gk. strophaligs "whirl, whirlwind," streblos "twisted").

STILL LIFE W/ CREOLE TOMATOES

I still live on the side of my life
  that was there
    I thought was whole

my eyes ate a simile in the headlines:
"Like Bricks on Jello"
& the levees broke like rock 'n roll lyrics
& I ain't got no Creole tomatoes
just hungry haunted blues
& my dog Orpheus lies dying

still life beside me dogging my etouffe blues
Thanksgiving in a city care forgot
FEMA forgot
post office forgot
post Katrina blues
no Creole tomatoes
just camouflaged humvees
military police at the Notre Dame seminary
Our Lady of Creole Tomatoes
seminal blues where the fruit & vegetable truck
used to stay on Carrollton Avenue
with those Creole tomatoes

I bought a $10 box right before Katrina
took those Creole tomatoes w/ me to Hattiesburg
ate those Vienna sausages w/ my Creole tomatoes
for a week w/ no power no water no CNN

didn't know the levees broke
didn't know the Superdome blues
the convention center blues
didn't know news

& Orpheus w/ golden glowing eyes
was headlining osteosarcoma

limping around those pine trees
while I was pining for Creole tomatoes
—banana & palm trees, mimosa & hibiscus—
the last bite a sacrament
holy Creole tomatoes
succulent nostalgia like crawfish
swimming in toxic gumbo
levitating ghosts eating coffin flies

I want my still life w/ Creole tomatoes
my whole dog Orpheus
w/ a whole leg not an egg of bone cancer
growing like a stuffed Creole tomato
fried green gangrened
coffin flies gathering like locusts

I am still in my life w/out Creole tomatoes
a gulf of despair: hurricanes w/ greek names in November
I remember the side of my life
still w/ Creole tomatoes
a casserole of hope:
I Eurydice & Orpheus looked back
to the poetry of Creole tomatoes
fetch me back too

to my life still full w/ Creole tomatoes
no similes brewing
to metaphors stewing
like my life still as August 26th
Orphan pup's 11th birthday
catastrophe 3 days away

now it's December the winter solstice
stalking the city like a hungry jaguar:
Orpheus is dead
the cancer ate him up &
it's Christmas in a city care forgot
FEMA forgot, post office forgot:
my last sacrificial gift:

ashes in a floral etched silver urn &

this ain't no story written on jello

Note: Hurricane Katrina struck New Orleans Aug. 29, 2005. When levees broke the city was flooded.

KATRINA KRISTMAS

Last year I returned from the gulf coast
after the family gathering
to witness snowflakes
"real snowflakes" I recall telling my mother on the phone
like the ones in New Rochelle where I grew up
before the family moved south
the summer of '64 to Greenwood, MS
the summer of Mississippi burning
when my mother went to a grocery
& the clerk aimed a rifle at her
"what are you doing here yankee"

Last Christmas silvery metallic snowflakes
each geometrically unique fell against my cheek
burning individual designs exquisitely true
the day before the tsunami that shifted the earth's axis
minutely fractile perfectly invisible to the naked eye

This kristmas I stayed home in New Orleans
no visit to family—too depressed after orpheus
no gifts, just hollow gasps of breath
family on the coast in Ocean Springs
after the phone call to brothers, parents, nieces, nephews
after the gossipy news

I took my hollow form
out on the back deck
the sky turquoise
the sun brilliant gold
the silver & amethyst
pendant & earrings
burning my cheeks & breastbone
searing them with healing heat
my eyes drinking in the swirling energy

wishing the fence would finally be built
so my 3 remaining dogs could have a yard
thinking of the golden glowing amber eyes of Orpheus
golden retriever, put to sleep 2 weeks ago
his remains in a silvery etched urn
burning hollow grief
relief in this katrina kristmas
I sit on the deck trying to heal my hollow depression
with thoughts of golden gems: citrine, topaz, amber, carnelian
eyes glazed with light/with life

& I look sideways at the almost lifeless orchid
left 6 weeks without water everything dried up
& moribund when I returned from Hattiesburg in October
no rain—as if the healing was predestined—
the damn purple orchids are about to burst
with amethyst enthusiasm
out the spastic stalks

I am inside now in shadows writing this poem
I think about my friend today who needs healing
blood spurting from her mouth & nose
strokes, blood thinners, her topaz hair
the friend who called 8am sunday August 28th
& said category 5 get the hell out
probably saved my life & my dogs & cats
not orpheus though, the cancer already spread
throughout his form, earthly congregation of organs,
this katrina kristmas is only what it is:
pure energy recollected in tranquility.

My house is not yet healed, my soul wrecked
not decked in silver & amethyst, lights glimmering
invisible colors are tattoos across this listless day.
I wait for whatever may come, I wait for peace
on earth, I wait
for the damn orchids to bloom.

STOCKING STUFFERS - Christmas Day 2006

my younger brother's fourth wife stirs
marshmallows into the chocolate delight.
'twas the night before xmas when all thru the house
Bing Crosby wafted "I'll be home for Christmas"
like potpourri to camouflage emotional stench
of decades' angst—home and what is home?

she mixes and tosses and grates her first
two marriages, son. I always liked the first
wife best, though best it was they split.
now all four of us, my three brothers & I
in the same decade—fifties—parents eighties
pushing ninety, my father's alzheimer's creating
repetitive litanies of forgotten links - poems
of dislocation, collating lost images,
family photos. salad is ready, layered
with despair and other concoctions.

glad I skipped all that, though I did exercise
my constitutional right to choice several times
in the '70's and '80's—but this poem
is not about politics. It's about mixing metaphor
and emotional goo into something
edible—editable?

under the tree of our lives brightly colored packages
are exhumed, distributed, ripped open by claws
of Christmases past, present and what is to come?
Nieces and nephews from sublevels, subdivisions
of familial bondings, divorces, are held together by
dances of sugarplums, ipods, cellphones, keys to
convertibles—pacifiers in this electronic age -
it's us babyboomers who fucked up—but we were
born of war and lost our innocence in another war.
But this poem is not about politics—it's about rage.

I want to take marshmallow chocolate delight
and shove it up Santa's ass - all the Christmases
past and present—families on the gulf coast
homes gutted and devoid of memory—blank.

Last year, katrina kristmas, didn't visit family
on coast, a ghost of xmas past, this year
ghosts of childhoods gone, parents going to move
into house on farm of another brother,
brother (with 4th wife going to move to North Carolina)
soon broken pieces of home, like homemade candy,
consumed by holiday hunger and joy, hunger and joy—
the gulf coast ravished, New Orleans
raped by politicians, left for dead with nothing to celebrate:
tell me why I am supposed to be comforted with joy.
I forget, in the city of care, I forget that I want to drown
my joys in this city. this city that I call home...
bittersweet home ... I stir.

WINTER TREES POST-K

> *"On their blotter of fog the trees*
> *seem a botanical drawing"* – Sylvia Plath

bent over like vultures
the trees broken-backed
stalk my backyard through a steeple
of churched branches

gothic view through curved ovals
the church lurches vividly wise
visibly cursive my eyes'
selectivity: withering heights
of broken edges, birds' eggs
not hatched, doves nesting in potted plant
by back door—my yard usually thronged
by banana trees, lizards, dragonflies,
butterflies: my golden retriever Orpheus
tells the animal psychic, remember me
when butterflies spin my bones into cancerous
cyclones after Katrina's wrath, wraithlike
I hover dragonflying between plastic squeaky toys
Pandora his golden sister ransacks the lizards
native to Florida who claimed my yard after the deluge—
squirming raccoons bespectacaled, confused
retching, wrenching away from the three remaining dogs
circling like wolves, where o where have the habitats gone
no more snakes, thank god, writhing from the river
the rankled, broken, wretched branches
torn and storm-ridden sculptures laugh
at the season's sappy endings:

I swoop down my hungry eye to gulp every lurid branch.

WINTER TREES 2007

lizard crouches on table edge
visiting from another galaxy
after katrina
birds caw, screech
moondog wimpers wanting out
new fence gnawed on like chewy bone
clouds crunch down blue of sky
vine strangled winter tree sprung
with cat's claw, kudzu, spanish moss
at river's edge
windchimes chime mississippi melodies
outside of time i am outside of
see what happens if i camouflage
muddy skin with greenish shimmers:
will i snare an insect with my twisted tongue?
will i garnish a meal with wintergreen?
lizard vanishes into light or dark:
it is winter and i pine for spring
blue sun risking everything.

ATTACK OF THE CREOLE TOMATO CATS

creole tomatoes festing
in the sun
they are almost done
ripening their souls
orange/red/yellow
gradients photoshopped
chopped by eyeballs
alive dancing in the light

my black & white cats'
energy senses their presence
in the brown paper bag
nesting in my purse
casually strewn on the couch
they crouch domestic stalkers
nightshade elementals
round orangey victims
tiny bites, claw marks
dent the asymmetrical fruits
toxic to cats
almost a halloween joke
all saints/all souls day

my dogs chase the cats
monochromatic rainbows
I am solemn and aware
something has shifted:
the creole tomato truck is back

in front of notre dame seminary
on carrollton avenue
seminal visions/new precedents
new president
katrina all souls damaged
shadowy gustav pales
contraflow a politicians'

trompe l'oeil moment
tricky assumptions
my angel cat ariel attacks
this poem, pale scythe of claws

there is a new order
of creole tomatoes marching
their flambeaux's into my eyes'
lambent directions—iris'
dilated gaussian blurs
glaucoma, cataracts
graduating in the afternoon sun.

I will slice them into succulent mandalas
pepper them with cilantro and blue cheese
a soupcon of vinaigrette
consume them, floating rapturously
down throat/esophagus
gyrating images pasted onto papery tongue:
new orleans is safe again
the guardian creoles of levees
sainted, scented tomatoes levitate
right before my eyes.

my dappled cats give glory to god
for toxic things to attack
my dogs just are
it's november and a hurricane
playfully hovers over cuba.
my creole tomatoes are basking
in the sun: light: ripening.

KATRINA UKHUPACHACUTI
a transformation of reality by means of water

"all changed, changed utterly/A terrible beauty is born" – Yeats

serpent, jaguar, hummingbird, eagle:
Incan and Mayan legends foretell the end of time
time erased when the calendar ends
blue water-words float along chakras & spines
the serpent pines for your intestines
jaguar wants your throat
hummingbird your heart
eagle your spirit

the end-time is here heralding
the end of:
Cartesian time:
vanishing points don't vanish,
western history & religion blown away
by organic no-time-space continuum
all space-time one moment now

Katrina ukhupachacuti transformed
this crescent city into galactic butterfly
infinity spiraling dna
pluto on the galactic center
edge of black hole wisdom serpent
the big easy is out of time: of
FEMA time
Republican time
political merry-go-round fraud time
poor and disenfranchised time
lives & houses in toxic gumbo time
stir it all & ladle out the end of time–
end time: in the city that time forgot
reality transformed by breaking levees
by means of water

Mayan Tzolkin day 2 Cib (vulture/wisdom)

a good day to sit on a rock & contemplate
ancient memories from sacred sites/
sights: mississippi serpent winds down
north to south huge watery boa constricting
squeezing out liquid time into the gulf
Mexico to Peru: it will eat hurricanes
exploding spirals of energy—luminous cyclones
cycles of reality transformed globe
latitudes circling awareness
today Caban Earth keepers of the garden
displaced from time & natural cycles
quakes of emotion, tsunamis of fear:
this beautiful crescent garden is back

transforming consciousness, brain cells
reality as we know it swallowed by
personal memories, myths, the past:
reality by means of water,
transformed. *the big easy* out of time
ahead of time, the waters of time
healing the myth, turning everything
upsidedown insideout tiny city in a snow globe
shaken for its beauty, shaken to its knees
praying like hell, transformed utterly.
reborn.

ALL SOULS
ALONG THE MISSISSIPPI

Composed on the Back of a Dark Green Muddy Waters' Poster

When I woke up on the batture
& you were not only gone
but had never been there
& I heard the aluminum
silence of the river
I was scared –
It wasn't *metaphysical*
exactly
I just thought they were firing
cannons over the water
to make Huck's carcass rise

– Everette Maddox

MUMMINGS

mistress of flames
lady of strength
& writings of Thoth himself
she is within the cavern of her lord:

"Clother" is her name
hiding her creations
carrying away hearts:

hacker in pieces in blood
lady of flame
she is holding an inquisition
of the bandaged feeble one.

adapted from E.A. Wallis Budge, trans.
of **The Egyptian Book of the Dead**

styling my head into a wet relief
soothes, cools, nulls &
the hands of the hieroglyphs
shift me with cloth
into secreted wrappings.

at first Lon Chaney, Price,
Karloff, Lugosi THE MUMMY
stir images: dots of mytho-beginnings
in televised youth: the pyramid
crumbling dust asphyxiates curses
the eye (of RA) through a screen
of ancient herbs & alchemical mixes: the hand

she is holding an inquisition
hacker in pieces in blood writings

this choking dryness—
unremembered

during the setting in
the saying of words
from the book of the dead—
in the time of drying out
forgets the wetness
thrilling my nerve
stopping the dendrites & ganglia
on their ways through halls
& hidden doors: Isis unveils

she is holding an inquisition
of the bandaged feeble one
only the wet hands of cloth
mark my conscious thought
stirring unguents & must powders—
pores stuffed with anaesthesia chill
as I lie on a slab dying
by profiled by symbolized
hands

whose lines can't be read
whose force is flat
dulling a system
closing doors, passages
locking things in.

she is holding an inquisition

the dry part comes on
pinching my lungs
snuffing out air &
my image is carved above me
on the sarcophagus:

that I am dead film curled up
like vine shoots from a grave
passes my brain through atrophy
like chalk marks uncoding
windings of dna strands.

consciousness come harder
at the dying than ever:
my vegetable nerves start
stalks of asparagus fingers
toes bunched radishes &
legs of unbent wheat: breasts
bitten by holy scarabs peak &
my guts involve all until
surfaces matter not at all.

razors scrape & slit the spine
cutting cords lines of contact
unhook belief in pain instilled
belief in afterlife cursed &
warded off with poison glyphings:

may I rise even I (even eye)
may I gather myself together
like a hawk beautiful of gold
with the head of a phoenix
entering to RA

may be given to me
divine wheat for my mouth
may I obtain power through myself
over the keeper of my head
            (Book of the Dead)

none of that happens:
I remain intact.
they incant me
the way to sleep:
to feel & then let loose
body parts so that nothing
but floating matters.

instead I curl
tight like a snail

moving along the ridges
of my shell:

outpecking my shell
outfating the phoenix
I shout back after her
Thel! Thel!
but lose sight of her

the bandaged feeble one

when I feel the stirrings
of hands outside peeling
back the layers crusted & powdery
I am ready for it:

the final cloth is pulled
back from my eyes
the light blazing blinds
for a moment my eyes
& I stiffly move a foot
forward & fall
to a brittle clutch
on the doctor's knees:

my knuckles sprout
onion white
in my eyes
which I raise & raise
& the Nile jerks up
its flat head
like a cobra ruled
by leveled flutings:

may I gather myself together
divine wheat for my mouth

may my head end
without the curse of RA-Chaney

may my eye be healed
to rub out Karloff's face
may Lugosi not grab
my feet troll-like
from under my bed.

may I obtain power through myself
over the keeper of my head

may tears rinse & rinse
from the ducts of the sphinx.

DUTCH BOY'S FINGER

> *"Over again I feel thy finger and find thee"*
> *-- Gerard Manley Hopkins*

I inhabit a pink shotgun
on a bend of the mississippi's mouth.
it engulfs me like an amoeba or jonah's whale,
intestinal home

whose windows blink in rhythms of prisms
& colored bottles: hamlin's wizard oil,
brown ginger tonic, blue bromo-seltzer,
hood's sarsaparilla—cure any ailment
of body or spirit:
rubber & jade & pencil plants, peacock feathers
snake images, stashes of unused poems, mardi gras beads --
aggregations of my objective life.

my sun registers in the earth
container of things
while air ascends & pulls
me apart stretching
endlessly my rubber ego
& only a fingertip keeps its midpoint
from giving out.

the weight of these things presses me down
like ocean waves' impersonal tonnage
& trying to breathe is as impossible
as getting out of bed, as Diane Wakoski said
'I want to go to sleep and never wake up' --
but dreams are just as troublesome & more real.

an ex-lover's ghost glimmers against these walls
as shadows cast from the blue blue scented genie lamp
& up on the levee dutch boy
plugs the hole w/ his finger —
divine finger owning a saint's patience

a buddha's third eye.

the philosopher's stone must be this finger
if he takes it out
the world will turn insideout, expelling
& shrivelling like a balloon or a stomach.

being outside is unbearable.
on the streetcar
a man in a gray flannel suit touches
my blue-jeaned knee.
the mailman returns me to the book of the month club
& a file of cockroaches follows me to the river
unfooled by my piping, flawlessly alive.

dutch boy, just keep your finger in
this pied world
or the molecules will all fly off like blackbirds
unlimiting things
unfitting kings.

dutch boy, when you touch me
are you holding me back
or letting me out?

dutch boy, you could scour my doorstep
w/ your trigger finger.

IMBOLC

for my father July 6, 1917-February 2, 2011

1.

Your metamorphosis was the midpoint
of the winter solstice
& the vernal equinox—
you fluttering midway
between dementia & clarity—
galactic butterfly entering
the black hole in the center
of your galaxy
precession of the equinoxes
spelling time backwards
out of order
out of time
the world clock
stops

you midway between
frigid death & burning rebirth
between stillness & movement
out of your hole on St. Brigid's Day
(turned by pious Christians
from pagan fire healer
& goddess of poetry
to self-sacrificing saint)
you didn't see your shadow

self
this last Christmas in the nursing home
on the Mississippi gulf coast
the first and last time I saw you there
eating Christmas dinner off a paper plate
at a table with a gray
almost coherent Mrs. Smith

alone with strangers
not home with family
weather too bitter and rainy
mother feeling under the weather.

The last time I saw you
tried to explain that I would be 62
in January & applying for social security.
You ask the same question over & over:
why I took the buyout from the paper
in New Orleans—finally you get it
& ask "how did we get so old"?
a moment of lucid combustion—
you a shadow wavering over
your family
freezing the phrase
in my crystallized brain.
I cry on the way out—
the last time I will see you
your cocoon of fire
a chrysallis
about to collapse
into ashes
at the national cemetery in Biloxi.

2.

Curling old photographs with serrated edges
in black & white of course
faded from the '50's
not your digital jpeg's
in high resolution
I rummage through the box
my mother gave me decades ago
"how did we get so young?"
My father trim and dapper
swashbuckling, even.
there is one of my grandmother
Nana on the porch of our Lake Champlain

cottage in upstate New York
at the bottom my father's handwriting:
"unquestionable serenity"
a quest I didn't know he was on:
I always remembered that photo
with the words "absolute serenity"
& was shocked to find the clumsiness
of "unquestionable" weighing
on the bottom of the photo
weighing my memory:
our relationship always stormy
oppositions and squares
tsunamis & hurricanes
me the renegade poet amongst
doctor and engineer brothers,
black sheep, the milk of the ewe—
Brigid's legacy of Imbolc fires.

my grandmother a conflagration
of aggravation in the roaring '20's
shimmying party girl alcoholic who came to
christian science in her later years
my father perhaps mortified by his
mother's wild ways sees her
"unquestionable serenity" a blessing
not a quenching. When he was born
women didn't have the right to vote.
he wanted to fight the Spanish Civil War
but Nana wouldn't let him go & throw
away his life for a just cause, or just a cause.

In later years my cousin Vivian would be
a union organizer for Cesar Chavez—
women who run with the wolves—
whale riders, fire priestesses,
no room for serenity there.
Howling at the moon, bloody menses
smearing the photos with red.

Dismembered Sedna refracting
rainbows of betrayal
by draconian father
marries her dog instead
of chosen husband, career
pushed out of the boat
hand chopped off
torso, limbs in uterine limbo
abused mermaid drowning
in the amniotic fluid
rejects tradition, her role sacrificed
by submerged desires
ugly undine underwater dramas
breeched fire-breathing dragons
reborn with ceremonies
at the equinoxes, afterbirth burned.

When my father enlisted in WWII
he never went overseas, his watery blue eyes
weakly wavering behind glass lenses
kept him on terra firma, USA.
St. Brigid breathes fire on Imbolc
ashes resting near the beach
where a gulf encroaches.

3.

Deathwatch a wallpaper of CNN coverage:
while I wait for my father to die
patriarchal dictatorships are collapsing
desecrated mummies & distant pyramids pillaged
middle east & north africa erupting
throngs protesting decades' wrongs,
military rules, bloodbaths
& I wait for my father
to die, to end his regime, let truths & lies
be bygones: the obituary my younger brother
wrote does not mention his first wife—
the reason my twin brother & I were adopted.

I have the faded black & white photos
of a woman holding us with my father there,
a shaggy terrier looking on.
My reality swept under oriental carpets
on my grandmother's floor, us crawling
around, exploring our myths. I still keep
an empty brown leather jewelry box
my father gave me to remember—
I have the proof.

The butterfly effect of Imbolc:
my father dies
a whole continent in chaos,
dying histories
cultures shocked, new futures
hovering over flames and funerals
volcanoes spewing ashes
earthquakes creating tsunamis
of guilt & repression,
from the center of the galaxy
goddesses tending hearths
keeping flames burning
nurturing dysfunctional families
continuance of centuries
the social network toppling old lies.

My father dies & I wait
for outcomes, for social security
for some kind of serenity
while the world cracks & groans
& shifts tectonic plates.

I wait for my history to write itself
ashes to ashes, blood will tell.
I wait for a shadow
which can only be seen by
flames of the sun —
a fire goddess flings her arms
around the searing spring equinox:

solar flares disrupt
& we're still rotating
while you rest in peace
absolute serenity
just another myth, another story
foreshadowing ... the sound & fury
of rebirth.

God knows the shadow knows
the daughter knows the shadow

THE LOTUS-EATER GETS HER JUST DESERTS

aridly sitting here in my onyx
green silky oriental impressed-
with-jacquard-mandalas rayon
kimono, studded with pink-toned
embroidered roses
I'm listening to the blues
& thinking about past lives

a very mysterious shaped
suggestive succulent offshoots
its phalanxes of cucumbered destiny
beyond the tacky-but-beloved pseudo
art nouveau wrought iron lamps
implanted with glass prisms
through which I see that strange
unnamed growth:

I can't decide whether I should
or shouldn't
take on this task
or the task of moving
my ideogram-clad figure
to the kitchen for another glass
of quite dry white bordeaux

quelle idée
triste! my crystal petal
pillar-stemmed receptacle is empty
& I'm broken up about it.
break, please.

perhaps a full grail & two more of them frozen
eggrolls & I'll chant myself to sleep:
what could be easier in this pagoda of distraction?
ancestor worship just doesn't get it
especially since I was adopted
& have no fucking idea

but what the hell:
"I'm so blue I don't know what to do/
but please don't lay down & die/
there's so many more lifetimes a followin' you"
chant the speakers

& maybe my last life hid behind paper
wall-dividers riced with terrible condiments
I just don't know
but even this one is spiced with secret recipes
who deserted mother
who couldn't set the table & serve the courses?

I don't know what motive began this one
so how can I understand a poem's conception
riddled with shudders of miscarriage
in the thick of it? give up?
I've borne as much as I can.
the blues soothe me, my nerve endings
& spine. I hope I dream well tonight
of tusk-heaving trunked up elephants trudging
through streams of cobras in Indian jungles
forming 8's of lemniscates around my jugular
fluted throat:

THE DREAM: in the floating
wood pentagram coffin my grandfather
long dead anyway, lay frozen
I walk down the pier & climb aboard
it was all like a row boat peacefullydown the stream
& merrily, merrily I disembowelled him, reserving
the major organs for preserving in canopic jars
what jams we get ourselves in!

the scene intones hieroglyphic modes
& I place ceremonially the guts
into decorated amphoras while I sacrifice
certain ordained objects from my life
valuable & imbued with magic, spelled phylacteries

(the ceramic sun-child astride the horse,
sunflower emblazoning his hand, 3-D trump)
inside the star-shaped sarcophagus
I don't want to, I start
to take them out but think better
& my mother, his daughter
approves
I am selfish & don't want to give anything up
but am tempered by return
but am tempted by reward
it is my inescapable duty
there is no danger of loss
my mother comes down for inspection
of the finished task
as we float against an ocean of water
as an earthquake of land engulfs us

I am somebodies' daughter
in this life, in the next

song of the himalayas, sandalwood sifting
through this room's incensed memories
perhaps the cool-headed jasmine tea will lull
me into a deep sleep
protected by dreams' tricky folds

I hope my plants survive the winter.
tomorrow I'll enchant them
& maybe revise this:

my kimono, full of exotic lines
sinks & softens against my silken skin
brushed with prophecies I hold
in the palm of my hand

WOMAN CLOTHED WITH THE SUN

For Helen Toye 1940-2012

*"And a great sign appeared in heaven: a woman clothed with the sun,
with the moon under her feet, and on her head a crown of twelve stars."*
-- Revelations

*``Bring them down from their ruddy gallows;
Let there be clean linen for the backs of thieves;
Let lovers go fresh and sweet to be undone,
And the heaviest nuns walk in a pure floating
Of dark habits,*
    keeping their difficult balance.''
    —*Richard Wilbur*

August 18, 2012

It's your birthday
Almost four months after
You turned to ashes, ashen

you were curled around yourself
veinless alabaster whiter than
the crumpled nursing home sheets

the rainbow striped vase of roses
a shocking hue of reddish pink
my hands shaking uncontrollably
as I added water in the sink

your death slammed all my senses
at once: a fetal apparition
with tubes protruding
a bog person from the ice age
I cried when I held your bony fingers
my salty tears riming the ancient mariner

I think how we met in graduate school

at Tulane all those decades ago
where you had just arrived from
breaking down at Kent State
dead students too much pain

you could never take the pain
but you could transform it
into poems and paintings
your first show at the Loyola cage
rippling with rainbows of acrylic gyrations

the "Woman Clothed with the Sun"
your title work, your prismatic self-portrait
golden ratios of geometric proportions
lost now somewhere in a fire of purgation.

I bought the one I thought of as my Self
as I gasped with recognition
seeing my essence there—
a revelation not biblical but hindu:
arms reflected in the mirror multi-faceted
like a goddess, and the candle flaming
I saw as a shimmering cobra; you said
I was alive in the pointillist dabs of color,
& once in the early '80's I spent all
day on the floor (after swallowing an illicit
blot of paper harboring psychic disturbances)
and it was all around strands of moving
light undulating from the solar plexus
spiraling center circling the room endlessly
a beating heart—iambic pentameters
in a fourth dimensional color wheel
the aura of cancer in tortured black & white
cannibal cells eating each other.

At your funeral I tried to read a poem by Richard Wilbur,
"Love Calls Us to the Things of This World"
but my hands were shaking, my voice wavering
eyes watering:

Yet, as the sun acknowledges
With a warm look the world's hunks and colors,
The soul descends once more in bitter love
To accept the waking body ...

Helen, your life walked a "difficult balance"
your heart was the fulcrum, your art the mirror

now your urn rests with your husband's & you
are out of pain, as if pain were something in the pantry
like milk or bread or savory spices

your friends already on a karmic turn:
Robert, Dan, Everette, Carl, Jean, Hazel
who came to your earthly parties
opening into a cornucopia of food and wine
beef wellington, crawfish etouffee, black russians—
some here, some on the "other side"
of love,
revelations in a year of revelations ...

 Outside the open window
The morning air is all awash with angels

your dark angel painting, inspired by my dark angel poems of
Anael, still hangs on my chimney
darkly glaring at human follies

all the years of crashing our souls on the highways of passion
none of us felt mortal—we were poets and artists
living above the river's edge, the levees' overtopping hopes
desiring full spectrum filaments of the sun's flaming arms.

Yesterday floating in my pool I saw you through the branches
of the setting sun sending fragments of iridescent prisms
into my cataracts, my glaucoma'd iris' descent into dark
water lilies of lies and beauty, our only truth our lives.

You are clothed in fire, solar flair your costume for the ball.
we are all wearing white—gauzy apparitions—old friends
dancing around your maypole in a frenzy
swirling with angels, not going gently, but going with grace.

THE WIZARD WHO FELL TO EARTH AS FELLINI

The term "felliniesque" is used to describe any scene in which a hallucinatory image invades an otherwise ordinary situation...memory, dreams, fantasy, and desire, Fellini's films are deeply personal visions of society, often portraying people at their most bizarre. — Wikipedia

> **NANCY'S RIVIERA**
> On a pre-summer's day of beer, years ago,
> Two Michael's and I
> Put together your new swimming pool.
>
> The ladder of shaky bolts,
> We held it for each other's tipsy entrance,
> Trusting that,
> When the time came it would take us out.
>
> Thanx, Nancy, for being our ladder.
> – Robert Borsodi, from *Off On A Wonderful Ride*

Bob draped in white at Helen's Maypole party
eyes laughing at us goddesses in white cotton concoctions,
he is Fellini directing the perfectly absurd movie
of our bohemian madness
the clothesline pole transmogrified with white crepe paper streamers
we dance around it wine-filled nymphs - lecherous satyrs eyeing us
satiated with crawfish etouffee and beef wellington
Bob is in his element—all those hungry poets gorging, drinking, smoking
reading poems, dancing dances, singing songs

we were all there, extras from the Maple Leaf and
Borsodi's coffee house
Everette. Sara Beth, Dan Hughes, whose hues were purple
back from Ethiopia and Egypt
(he and Helen in my small above ground pool
Dan invoking Ra, the perfumed essences from Egypt
he bestows on us in the St. Charles mansion with rooms for rent

to arty types)

Bob in the Freret Street coffee house
directing plays, poetry readings under bizarre circuses of human play
(Everette and I ejected one night because we were rowdy and
laughing)
the doves singing, the decor topsy-turvy with Sara Beth's surreal
mania

when Bob comes over for dinner
he fixes things—hammer in hand under sink or pounding nails
in door sills
Sara Beth cleaning my kitchen (I am not a domestic diva)
we all gather in the round turquoise pool - installed by Bob
& other coffeehouse castoffs - for free food & booze
(that's all it took in those days)

the last time Bob & Helen Toye read at the Maple Leaf
he inscribed his chapbook:
"My brief poem to you on page two. Thanks for having me 'n Helen
this chilly Halloween Sunday", Love Bob 'n Karin
the poem about putting together the small round pool
which Everette dubbed "The Carrollton Riviera" the location
for our felliniesque gatherings under summer solstice skies—
(years later I would move to a bigger place, bigger pool
where older, we would still act like the younger fools we never left
behind!)

when I heard of his cancer and jump from the bridge,
a harlequined tarot card Fool leaping over the precipice
trusting voodoo bones into the care of the river
—river styx sticks in my brain—
my first thought, as I tripped over it
Bob fixed the door sill!
broken again after all these years—what "ladder of shaky bolts"
have you left us balancing on?

shocked & not knowing, not knowing about the cancer of the bones
arrows plunging into a watery hexagram of agony

the twinkle in wizard eyes a splintered prophecy

Bob always said he did not believe in anything hereafter
a few days later, as I get out of the shower
a projectile force thunks me on the head—
I am thinking about Bob in his existential unbelief—
see a small triangular piece of plastic cast on the floor,
check the light fixture, nothing missing
the force of projectile not in proportion to the tiny shard—
Bob are you trying to tell me you have reconsidered your philosophy?

At the Maple Leaf in November
Karin, his final love, arranges a memorial reading
it goes on into dark, dark, dark
felliniesque fade-outs, juxtapositions of time & shadows

she gives me a gift—a framed photo of Robert the summer before
a trip through time & foretold space:

red glowing room w/ guitar and pinball machines
coca-cola sign and long white beard—
foreshadowing scene—months before his demise
disguised as grim reaper, scythe in hand
or is it pen, nepenthe, forgetfulness—purgative of sorrow

I tell Karin about the triangular assault in my bathroom
she says I am not nuts—for a week or two after his great leap
cushions and objects were flying around the coffee house
a frenzy of communication, magical wizardry—yes, yes, yes
there is life after death! a ritual was performed
Tibetan book of the Dead, Bob convinced to go home,
Merlin back to crystal cave, long white beard flowing, eyes glinting
with new knowledge he's passed on to us, leaving the gift
to unwrap, unravel, unrevel, revealing an ordinary situation
death after life after death after life extraordinary ....

Thanx, Bob, for being our ladder

MY DOG COMES TO THE WORD "DEATH"

   for Mandrake

death. death. death.
death. death. death. death. death.
if you repeat a word often enough
it becomes meaningless
just the hollow sound of a foreign tongue
you can't follow:
thump-thump, thump-thump, thump-thump-thump.

that being the noise Mandrake
beat out on the hardwood floors
clicking the cliches

in the middle of the night when I couldn't sleep
& he had ticks & fleas to scratch
& I had sheep to count:
one, two, three, four, five
da-da, da-da, da-da, da-da
throbbing heartbeats alive
with the backbone of poetry:
iamb, therefore I shrink.

here, Mandrake, here, Death!
his ashes are hermetically sealed in
in a shockingly small
pale green celadon urn
draped with a garland of lotuses
faintly etched
his photographs propped around it
various crystals from the mineral kingdom
guarding the circle of fire.
when I hold its cold roundness in my palms
I cry, disbelieving the gleaming brown eyes
pouring unqualified, unconditional love
from the polaroid above
are dead

dead as my friend Everette, the poet.
a year for deadness. my job is dead. a love is dead.
once, many years ago, after a poetry reading
some writer friends came home with me
to eat red beans & rice & we typed out
tap-tap, tap-tap-tap
an exquisite corpse on my smith-corona.

Bob Stock was there & he's dead too.
that's when Everette grabbed Mandrake's box
of flavored dog biscuits & joyously
munching on a handful, washed it down
with swigs of scotch.

Mandrake set up a howling protest,
his eyes mournful,
so we gave him some biscuits, too
his favorite being the pale green ones.

now, many of my best friends are in heaven
& many of them are here.

which way do I turn for comfort?
tick-tock, tick-tock, tick-tock, tick-tock

MEMENTO MORI: THE BLACK BOX

for Everette Hawthorne Maddox

Your jazz funeral
was Black Orpheus
only a different
continent
a different rio
but the same old
carnival

the invisible skeleton
with hollow grin
ran unexposed, parading
through the crowds
clacking & clanking
with arrhythmic jerks
smoldering behind
every mourner's eyeballs

we drank
it all in, the dirge
of sounds, blue notes
the high balls
marching with unregimented
asymmetry around the corner
to a different bar

returning to a wake of free booze
& freely flowing tears
in the red tin rooms
of the Maple Leaf Bar
your only home for years

the black box: a ridiculous reminder

ashes to ashes & so it goes

put that in your pipe & smoke it
the black box
the night before
posed self-consciously
on Fred & Jenny's mantle
the tape recorder with your voice

coming out of another black box
& one of your drunk Alabama friends
picks it up & shakes it:
"Yup, it's Rette alright"
black humour that breaks the ice
in our drinks, in our souls

I pour a symbolic scotch
choking on its acrid taste & toast
you in the black box
haunting the mantle

wraith-like even in life
you constantly reminded us of death,
Everette, & love

the day we took you in the black box
the sky was bluer than it ever had a right to be
the day we took the black box
the sun so sharp its edges cut through us
the day we took you in the black box

down to the river, the beautiful, beautiful
muddy-brown, garbage-strewn river
yes, let us gather at the river
the day we took you in the black box
a month after you turned invisible
(except to Rosemary, who, a week later
saw you wavering, dandy like in your best suit
pipe & bar scotch in hand
in the doorway of Muddy Waters;
except to me: one night while watching TV

I felt engulfed by a palpable stench
of scotch incensing my livingroom;
except to Julie, whose Tarot reader said:
your friend doesn't believe he's dead yet
& he's pissed off)
I don't believe you're dead yet
& I'm pissed off that you can't feel
how the air changes around your skin
when a hurricane looms, how the sky
shifts, turning ominous & exciting

the day we took you in the black box
zigzagging through Carrollton streets
to the levee by the river, Mark Twain's river
Huck Finn's dreams, paddling through dark
muddy waters, now polluted with shiny cans
& golden brown beer bottles, portending
your next book's title, *American Waste*

six of us gathered at the river
beautiful, beautiful, muddy-brown, garbage-strewn river
whose sibilant name called you home: Miss-iss-ippi
where Dusty plunges into the muck, arm stuck up
like an Arthurian knight, keeping the black box out of the mire

rotting brown logs bobbing up & down
releases your ashes

into the river's mouth & we hope
the gulf stream carries them
somewhere south to an exotic spot—
at least in opposite direction
to Alabama

we join hands in a circle
gathering around the empty black box
& we begin to believe in your death, in ours
& in the miraculous blue sky

RESCUING MR. REDBONES

for Bill Maddox,
(April 25, 1949-March 31, 1998)

Nine books or nine hats
Would not make him a man.
I have found something worse
to meditate on.
             "Crazy Jane on the Mountain", W.B. Yeats

your last cat, Lazarus, didn't have a warranty.
it expired before schedule, before even the first
of nine lives wore out, before hairballs.
you always said none of your cats ever lived long.

last night it was March. it rained.
they called and said you were in the hospital.
you spit up black bile. your pulse was lost in space.
they found it somewhere on the ninth moon.
you were comatose. that was Monday.

I didn't want to deal with it. I went
home from work & sat out under the stars
on my deck, dogs and cats keeping me attuned,
I blocked it out. not serious, a minor condition,
you'll come to my next party, we'll laugh.

I was tired and stressed. Go to sleep early.
don't even check voice-mail or e-mail.
when I go to lock up for the night
I hear a scampering across the roof. The clear roof
slanted across the deck.
and there he is.
Mr. Redbones gold-tabby,
my psychic tuned-in cat,
who, when Mandrake died in '90,
kept vigil with me all night
over my faithful sandalwood dog
there he is—Mr. Redbones the archetypal cat,

whose name is an alchemy:
Mr. Bones, Henry Pussycat and Leon Redbone
changed into a sissy, scaredy-cat up on the roof
his adventure gone awry, bravery forgot,
panic set in, reason forgone.
he couldn't climb down.
I get the aluminum ladder. I entice him with roast beef.
he dines with gourmand pleasure, en pleine air, al fresco,
up on the roof.
I can't grab him, he'd claw me. I become subtle, observant.
subservient. I become tactical.
get the cardboard box with the catnip from inside.
bring it up the ladder. no way. trust me I say,
coaxing him with unconditional love.

no way. he creeps across to the lattice work,
hovering over the mandevilla vine.
fine I say, fine, just jump. jump into the box. no way.
losing patience, okay, asshole, you got yourself up there,
now come down the same way,

our eyes meet trust/distrust problematic compromise.
just jump Redbones, please, I love you trust me,
I won't harm you, please just jump. it's getting cold.
it might rain. please. our eyes lock.
he hesitantly puts one paw forward, then leaps
into trust. into love.
it wasn't so hard.
you're safe.
I'm tired. I want to sleep.

the next day was Tuesday, it was still March.
it was raining cats and dogs.

the news was bad. You are unconscious. I am numb.
I think about your brother Everette nine years ago
leaving us all surprised, out on a limb, treed soul.
it was yesterday. It was nine years ago.
I think about your last cat Lazarus. didn't even have

enough time for nine lives, nine mistakes, nine wives.

what was it you and your brother were scared of
in your small-town Alabama lives?
what childhood witch paralyzed you with fear
froze your will to make that leap
into the love & trust all cats tapdance to?
where was it ever written that you had to be famous?
there were no instructions, no formats, no divine will.
I see your eyes in Mr. Redbones, gambling trust for terror,
climbing down from isolated limbs.
you never woke up.
whatever liquid kept you numb
was clear and precise.
your liver exploded.

at the Church's Fried chicken
I drive by on the way to work
there's a sign that exclaims:
Just Arrived: Livers!
oh how the cats are caterwauling,
fucking & screaming.
Some are dreaming.

why Bill & why your brother, why couldn't you trust
some catnip in a box, some days of sorrow,
some rescuer worthy of your praise,
some of your nine lives scratchy & lusty & howling.

the next day was Wednesday. It was April. We were fooled.
you had died the night before.
the sun gripped the sky with foolish faith.
it grieved.
a gargoyle spitting up hairballs.
cats walk under ladders.
you are gone
and we have become superstitious:
nine lives, nine ladders, nine cats, nine moons—
poetry.

the wake will be at my house on a curve
of the Mississippi River, where we tossed
your brother's ashes nine years ago
almost to the day. My house now
where Bob Stock died and lived
where Everette lived briefly
where you have come to parties
with friends who loved you.

we would have caught you.

now April will pass and your 49th year
born in '49 will never multiply
seven times seven equaling
the number of days and prayers for the dead
in the Bardo Thodol, your mystery will mix
with the eyes of a cat,
gleaming chasing the dream
hunting the imaginary kill.

we would have caught you.

now your bones lie in Potter's Field
graveyard of the disinherited
a poetic enough end

what monstrous phantoms will
slap you on the back & say welcome
my friend, to eternal nonsense

the white light screeches
out of your soul's cat eyes
no saviour to bring you back

to life

we would have caught you.

UNEMPLOYED IN FALL

for Everette Maddox, 1982
"Life, friends, is boring.
         - John Berryman, Dream Song 14

I get up at eleven
in the equinoctial morning
light which slams the window
prisms against the walls
in lambent directions
only because a Jehovah's Witness
who sees the light & wants me
to read my bible rings the doorbell
assaulting my late-night eyeballs
but can he find me a job, not Job?

Idleness is the devil's workshop
was the metaphoric motto
of our purposeful Puritan forebears
who worshipped Good Hard Honest Work
but I pray to Idleness with Pagan Fervor
& ask it my forgiveness
ask it not to lead me into temptations
of nine-to-five wastelands
& my tarot reader deals me Justice & the Hermit
patience & solitude soothe me
as I assume the laid back docility of a lily.

Stayed out until 2 a.m. last night
taking communion in the local
tin-ceiling'd cathedral bar
pilgrimmed by unemployed poets
& poets who have jobs & just can't bear them.
We discuss a favorite dead poet's upcoming
birthday in Scorpio, ruling the House of Death &
Regeneration. I order more cheap white wine
& force myself to feel free. free!
out on a Tuesday night with no thought

for tomorrow, but when's Saturday?
The days of the week fade into nameless
moods of monotony & the tooth of time
is yanked from my alas poor yorick skull .

So Job died, being old and full of days.

I fix coffee, write a poem, decide
to turn the radio on, go to line X at the unemployment office
right in the heart
of sleazy downtown wino district
& pray, coming & going, I don't get mugged
or worse, while I wait to file my appeal
along with a cross-section of down-and-out America
doing infinite Hail Red Tape penances.

I reread, randomly, a host of Dream Songs
& shake my head heavy with sorrow
for poor tormented Henry in his Dream House
of nightmares, permanently "disqualified for benefits"
no longer bored, barred bard, quite dead-O.
Soon, I know, the seven dwarves of dread
will break the spell & poof me back to work, heave-ho.

UNEMPLOYED IN FALL #2

for Everette Maddox 1992

A decade later you're dead
& I'm unemployed again.
some things never change.
some things are
forever.

this time I can't visit you
at the Maple Leaf, or is it
house of the rising sun?

actually at this point in my day
the sun is setting over my house
& you I imagine flying above
my roof in your Sunday best
coattails flying in the wind
a glass of bar scotch held aloft
never spilling any of your spirits
across Carrollton, Oak Street
the Riverbend & in your bird's-eye-view
the sky a blue fall luminescent painting
perhaps by Chagall:
some crows, bees, dragonflies
adding natural interest.

what's new? nothing much, here.
same old antique bottles, colored glass
& prisms still fill my windows with light
& fluctuating tones, patterns, shimmering spectrums.
& speaking of spectral matters, I miss you
& want to know what you do now to occupy
your unemployed days & nights beyond time?

this morning, once again, the Jehovah witnesses
came to my door, awakened by Guinevere's barking,
not the doorbell. & this decade Mandrake's dead

who was at my side, always loyal. This time
my joblessness is stranger, more surreal
& more real. will I ever work again?
can't even collect unemployment, just dust.

& speaking of dust, I've been dusting off old poems,
many written when you were still here, taking me back
to lost decades, not worth finding.

an old friend of yours, Sam, showed up at the Leaf on Sunday
just as drunkenly obnoxious as ever,
not hearing about your death
until recently:
coming back to haunt his past. let bygones be.

well, a few years later, he'll be gone, too
bones drenched in alcohol, formaldehyde,
whatever

found dead in his bed
& I won't even feel guilty
that I didn't answer
his last incoherent letter
that I'll put aside, shaking my head
fluttering, my tongue
forming the word "weird"

a hummingbird blurs for a moment
fuchsia, across my field
of vision

NEW ORLEANS: ALL SAINTS DAY

for Julie Kane

last night we masked
& went to the monster mash.
it was a surreal extravaganza
dreamt by Fellini, given by artists
in an old crumbling convent
conveniently located near the CBD.

two papier mache
skeletons fucking
mechanically held us in thrall:
rooms revolved optically, blue, red
black & white, pinwheeling frightening
fun. we left spirited
treated to fantasy
& relieved of sinful ennui.

Halloween became All Saints Day
later in the night at the Maple Leaf Bar
unmasking vulnerability, exposed
to occult influences both on this side &
the other. romance fizzled, led by horror
& unknown metaphysics, juxtaposed
constellations, ghosts.

spent All Saints morning hungover, fearful
headache warded off by my empowered crystal
cool quartz hand soothing my forehead
unfooled by mounting anxiety foretold by the palm.

I make split pea soup chopping & sacrificing
celery, carrots, onions, potatoes, parsley
& the pungent garlic toe
whose earthy perfume I love to sniff
off my fingers all next day—warding off
finicky lovers & god knows what demons.

November 1st & the white roses are blooming
in gargoyle profusion against the front porch.
I snip some with pinking shears
& look down the side yard
where I see one or two rose pink ones
scraggily trying to resurrect.
I collect them, entwining them
with the creamy ones in the round rosy glass vase
on the mantel of my rented home —
built, my landlady tells me in 1868.
so I present all the dead spirits at my address
with an incensed, fragrant bouquet—an altered gift
on all saints day to remind them to go away & stop
haunting us living ones who don't want to be
reminded.

my prayers, I hand over to the living
ignoring the raps in my wall.
I fall asleep early to disconcerting dreams
whose wormy symphonies dance to my lies.

my unclothed eyes rotate REM stelliums
& dutiful relatives all over the city
paint vaulted graves stark white.
astonished angels of naked stone archly
point to the skies

we are uncostumed, unloved & undead ...

PRECARIOUS

for Tom

Ah! as the heart grows older
It will come to such sights colder
By and by, nor spare a sigh
Though worlds of wanwood leafmeal lie;
And yet you will weep and know why.
           - Hopkins, "Spring and Fall"

you kept appearing at my door
& I kept sending you away.
what does this man with dark
piercing eyes, wife & kids
in another state —
this man who called me
Cassandra as I descended
the library steps —
want from me? the night
we became lovers

you caught me in a vulnerable state
lonely, sick in flannel gown
& quilted robe, you couldn't resist
asking: what's it like to make love
on your water bed?

precarious, I said

(considering the storm surges
& weather changes beneath
the undulating sheets)

I dress & at your apartment
I meet your mother (improper introductions)
later we return to my place
in raining, chilling November
& I pull us naked into the icy night

running & dancing in the backyard
you, thinking me crazed
we take to the water bed
stacking Beethoven sonatas on the stereo.

sixteen years later I think about how young
I was & insecure & when your estranged wife
intervened, long distance, you dropped me
like something radioactive
        what half-lives live on?

you were setting me up, cutting me out
a character in your stories —
I should have fought.

ten years afterwards, I see you again
forgetting the hurt & anger
we are both older, sadder, wiser
(finding the truth in all the cliches)
we are friends, exchange addresses.
I send you my Anael angel poems & you write back:
"Vatic" was the word you used.

I kept meaning to write back, then let things slide
lost your address, stacked up many more precarious
lovers & gave way to the usual clutter of everyday.

now seven years later my first book is published
& I envision your face when you open the brown package
I send as a surprise.
at the poetry reading — when the only friend I know
who would have your address appears unexpectedly
from out-of-town — I'm happy for the coincidence
& ask him for it:
he stares at me with blank shock.
"Haven't you heard, don't you know?"
"Heard what," I ask. "Tom is dead, died two years ago
in a car wreck. He was on his way down here."

later at home, slugging down brandy
crying for a man two years dead
who lived two years longer in my head
(so that's why he stopped writing,
I think, my brain stupid, numb)

the pivotal word, "precarious"
swings through my head, flashing back
sixteen years to the night
I heard banging on my bedroom window
terrified, ready to call the cops.
the next day I see you on campus
& you ask why I didn't open the window —
precariously — at 3 in the morning to let you in.
you thought it would be romantic. I said
you were lucky I didn't believe in guns.
now I sit here wondering if I'll ever find
your letter again in my layers of junk-time
& if things would have been different
if I had let you in through the window that night

how the water bed would have ebbed
(now I'm up in the air, a loft)
if it would have changed the weather,
the balance in the universe, the synchronicity
askewed to allot you life — now —
to have your eyes smile at my "vatic" lines
see-sawing on the precarious fulcrum
of this crazy playground.

LAST BACCHANALIA
AT THE CARROLLTON RIVIERA

for J.A.R.

Tonight I've watched
The moon and then
the Pleiades
go down

The night is now
half-gone; youth
goes; I am
in bed alone

—Sappho
Trans. by Mary Barnard

drinks in hand, disrobed, we plunge
into the round turquoise water
splashing the New Orleans' night
with divine drunkeness,
foreknowledge
playing in the city care forgot—
streets named after Greek muses
a Mardi Gras parade called Bacchus

laughing & naked, unconcerned
with neighboring eyes
hidden by elephant ears'
enormous green shadows,
fig leaves, althea blossoms,
I let the iridescent wet beads & crystals
drape my bare breasts with constellations
of sparkling light
our rippling nipples mirrors for
starry white flowerettes falling into the pool

drenched air, hungover musky vine smells

you admiring the effect, us water-beings
secreting unbearable pearls
we emerge glistening, hungry
raid the fridge, fix another drink
then unabating, gyrate unabashed
& still lustily naked
to the middle room of red cabinets,
pentagrams, angels & magic
put Walter Wolfman Washington
into the cassette deck
dance & laugh, dance & laugh
swirl, swirl, swirl
arms, legs, torsos
guess I'm quite a girl
my jewels jangling
counterpointing

the blues

you step back & look at me & though it's time
for bed — you say you can't,
nothing can happen
we can only be friends —
you reject this irretrievable moment
of pure bacchanalian trust

my brain clicks to the other morning
when sheets were churned like a twister
over my bed, around our hips
& our gasps were thunder claps
(my dream last Friday night of shooting heroin,
sticking syringes all over my body
must be coming true — fore-
knowledge of numbness)
so I climb up into the loft & pass out

of my body. when I wake at 5 a.m.
you are no where, you are gone
leaving my front door wide open

to anything wild & oracular
caving in.

the sullen bruised grapes of Orphic truth
are burst against my palette
tasting the sour, sorrow-grown colors of dawn
& already something alien & alive (like you)
is clawing itself unwanted in my womb.

last tango of blood & I am numb, numb
the pleasure inundating my brain with pain,
my guts wishing I weren't a poet
amanuensis for myths & crazy gods.
we must be sane. cups overturned
fortunes told, fools' gold.

I am in bed alone
wiping up revenge-splattered dreams with nasty swatches from
'foul rag-and-bone-shop of the heart'
as my uterus cracks open pried
by metal plumbing tools
releasing the past & future
tenses, menses
your image flows across
the stark white ceiling

as a skull-and-crossbones
floats over your cracked open head
I do not know

you are in bed alone.

CHARMED, I'M SURE
(CELTIC CROSS)

1. RAIDO/journey

journey of the soul
communion
reunion
journey charm
disarmed traveller
come to no harm

I teach my Self
to let go
the inward plunge
(cliff-dwelling heart)
requires
daring
a leap
        not of faith
but of quiet desperation —
actually a shove from
my best enemy —
'without contraries (there)
is no progression'

so. I must give you up.
let go. let you go
on your own journey
alone (or not)
but our karma must be broken
this go-round
laid to rest
'ain't nuthin' gonna change'
until the lessons
hard are heard
until the coin is tossed
& heads are up
payment received

debts canceled

submission to the itinerary —
we are poles apart
journeys end in destined hearts
no longer lovers, our minds meet.
no more phone calls, person-to-person
collect

2. URUZ/strength

sacrifice, the next draw
from oracular space
void, dark velvety bag:
strength to give up
what no longer works

growth, change
severing bonds

a new religion
I'm joining up:
'opportunity disguised as loss'

seven runes lead the way
out of catacombed claustrophobia

an abortion only turned an eager soul
away from this door
answering to some other perception
of embodiment

your brain submits to time's illusion
where will your journey end?
intersecting on a map, we paused, kept going.
they'll name a town after us: Hopelessville
will put us on the map. mad cartographers/
sane cartomancers
we took a chance

manhood, womanhood, a wild ox.

I need a new travel agent.
I'll ask for a brochure
at the next stop
from Lightyears Tours

3. DAGAZ/breakthrough

transformation, major shift
my axes reverse
a new age, an old hearse
an ancient, ancient curse

"nine books or nine hats ...
By the road an ancient cross ...
Gaity transfiguring all that dread"

Yeats, Celtic Poet Magician
heals woes & godknowswhat heartaches
daylight comes & can't be put off.

let's get on with it
veer down an unmapped road
straight into Chaos
& rejoice in getting lost

it comes with the territory.
terror resides behind a white picket fence

I am in full control
& worship Pandemonium
with meticulous ritual:

let's go, let's go. let go.

4. FEHU/possessions

nourishment
I eat, therefore I am
fullenough to feed you

we ate each other up
fast food love
& the rain forests were
sacrificed for our greed

you feed me lines
& I write them down

our love was so rare
the ozone layer disappeared
& now we live in wintry discontent
our hothouse blooms
brown & dried up.
possession leads to growth
not obsession

so I have come to learn
too late perhaps for us
but not for me, untied
by one half, whole

I have eaten of the tree
the branches are crooked
with divine messages runic cryptograms
the fruit of my labors

pressed with aching feet
fermented, now wine
I drink from the cup of your
toxic soul, solar plexus, nexus
of our poisoned fairytale

I get drunk

& give away everything
I own.

5. INGUZ/fertility

hero-god of new beginnings,
I hail you
whoever the hell you are.

or, are you moon-goddess
many-armed & liberated
woman of completions

a new breed
delivered from the past
ready to crack out of the egg
bursting the cocoon
a new species
(or, perhaps not new,
just forgotten)

retrieved from the earth's bowels
monolithic crystals
heaved up to teach us
the way out of here!

knowing you as father,
I can give birth to myself
over & over again
coiled around the world egg
hatching myriads of plots

at the place of four roads
intersecting
the rune sign waits
for travelers in the know.

the way is clear
there are no more rest stops

you must keep going to the end
of the line that never ends

or meets itself, embracing lovers.

6. PERTH/initiation

Unknowable Fool, full
of hidden meanings —
behind the veil of ritual
the eagle finds its mate
& incubates more mysteries

the unexpected Trickster waves
a wand to true North
encompassing what we don't
understand — our hearts
artfully graphic
writhing into knots of
jewelled snakes
biting with utmost bliss

an occasion of mystic fire
sacrificing what we fear to lose
our egos cracked open
to feed the newborn
mouths, myths

I trust you to sacrifice me
I want you
to leave me alone now
can you find your own way
back to your source
& acknowledge me sorceress
of your spell, undoing?

let's get on with it
& if we meet on some foreign train
at some seductive port

on our mutual journeys
we can have dinner & a chat
laugh about our cruel fate
the joke on us
how we devoured what we did not own.

I'll always love you — that's dessert.

7. ALGIZ/protection

rushes, eelgrass, elk babies floating on a river
in woven baskets
hold the mirror up to your newborn Self
seek protection from the Warrior Shadow —
a journey charm would be useful now.
be careful. know who you are.

know where you are & why.
claim your surveying tools
& trade tall tales of your prowess.
a protection pouch contains
a universe of selves —
feathers, crystals, bones,
snakeskins, seeds, little stones
oval, with crude markings.

new worlds arise for every need.
every danger averted is fraught with magic
medieval tales of gnomic mischief.
powers, powders of protection
stream through my fingers

that are making potions
that withdrew seven runes —
beginning with a journey
ending with protection,
a surprise!

upsetting developments

leave me breathless. leave me.

let's jump into the volcano
who knows when we'll get another chance
to get burnt. the gods will protects us
if it's their will, or whatever fickle
whim moves them. where that leaves us?

in the middle of absolutely nothing

circle of seven trees whose leaves
sprout glyphic veins & guard the seeds.

HARVEST MOON: FOOL IN THE POOL

for Ken Fontenot

lolling against the horizon
a pale off-white breast floats uneasily
bloated
waiting to be milked of some desirable
substance

the blood that drips haphazardly between
my legs
cramps into impossible graphics
& I gloat over revenge-worthy details
of careless days' futilities, delays

the flaccid fried eggs on my plate dotted
with globules of Tabasco
retain their glutenous outlines
in the presence of fire, dripping between
my fingers

when I step on the maverick sliver of glass
furious red blood rivers along the kitchen
linoleum, astounded with bloody footprints:
blood on the tracks, I muse
making tracks for the bathroom & bandaids
to dam the flow

manically the bloody mary lands on the floor
& I knock over my nerves

full moon in pisces opposing virgo sun
makes tracks across the sky's abdomen
& my virgin bitch Guinevere comes into first heat

upon arrival home from the world of getting & spending
my book, *The Compleat Astrologer,* is ravaged

by canine fangs & all is foretold backwardly
by dreams of horned wild boars & rhinos
mysteriously dog-sized & wearing collars & tags

so far the night hasn't finished waxing
& when the phone rings it's Ken who says
he's going to Germany on a grant
has written 500 poems in the past 3 years:
I say I haven't written a word in half that time.

so now I'm reaping & bleeding & trying to start the flow
stay the stain, harvest what I've pooled

the craggy quartz crystal records the discord
when I drop it to the wavering bottom:
I hold it up to my watery eyes
that gather in the lunar impulses
rippling with ripe, altered-state colors
& between my legs I'll soon see the reflected moon
float in miniature as I synchronize my starry limbs
swimming in the round turquoise
where I'm under its influence

dropping to the bottom of the sky.

HUNTER'S MOON

Full Moon Eclipse

these words appear upsidedown
a new darkside twist to dyslexia
& one moon ago I began the harvest
now I chase the metaphor
foxy lexicon
for the thrill of the kill

blood dripping out of gashed wound
gnashed teeth drooling saliva

things aren't that different: the quartz
still radiates its viscous parallels;
magnets still draw me to formed chaos;
screeching, scratching creatures fall prey
to saturnine structure; this moon-in-aries impulse
teaches me the truth of divisive neptuned illusion
opposing the harmonics of venusian manipulation.

I chart the sky's madness tonight without guilt
patterning across blackboard dreams: can a new
sequence begin after the solar eclipse in libra
balancing the delicate & dangerous question?

is Mme Blavatsky still alive & well & spelling in my ouija board
unceremoniously askew after I used it yesterday as a dustpan?

metaphors in everyday life:

from dust to dust: what IS the influence, confluence
of full moon rites
          rights
                    you should know, sower of manic seeds

you should teach
          knower of universal

dogcrap

bow wow WOW! writing again seems silly & razor-edge foolish
but the weather's turned sour, light's changed, saddened by time
turned downright moldy-green & last night I lit candles
incense ritualistically glad
for a new season of things to do, listless
 I ease these words onto this page like an egg
bravely onto the frypan, cracking open cellular
opportunities

what can I accomplish under this festering moon-yolked eve?

like as not I'll probably tear this up in the morning
or spill coffee on it
        after writing ad copy all day every day
for years & years & paying the dirty angel my wages, Mammon, shit-
head
buy this, it's a steal, it's ravishing, it flatters,
        it's polyester!
it will change your life, get you a job
        get buried in it

but I turn my back, turn to the powerful, passive reflection
of the sun's rays on an inanimate stone that looks yellow
& round & most suggestive
        for time untold

eonic fossils who once were bloody & squirming
& found solace under its magnetic appeal

I'd like stone to engulf me & this moment &
hibernate exclusively for about a few billion years

& turn up one day in the skeptical hands
of a rock hunter
        under a full moon's astral curse
                smearing me with ancestral blood

FULL MOON IN TAURUS

Dear Full Moon,

I begin this notorious note at midnight.
I may have some compromising collages to report
of lizards & snakes figure-eighting themselves
around each other to decorate square patio trellis.

glowing, crystalline I ready myself for sleep
hoping your rotund milkiness will suckle my dreams —
what nipples! mistress moon, huntress of blood
& howling dogs hovering over tranquil pools:
gypsies stumble drunkenly out of campfire circles
to predict catastrophe, denigrating fortune

all hung up on the hanged man's toe:

futile stick, the fool trips over the edge
cascading through the abyss, blissful smile
a halo on his lips. when I wake from lucid dreaming

to a morning of hazy coffee
magic wand with quartz-terminated ends
throws light around this prismatic sun-strewn room
& points the way to my Taurus North Node:
I conjure apollo
god of poesy & strutting drama
to appear at my electric
fingertips, tripping the words I prithee
tiptoeing typically across this keyboard — alpha to omega.

bull-headed full moon tenaciously grabs
me by my senses & turns them upsidedown
towards the objects that surround:
prisms half-heartedly
shaking weak sun through themselves
for a show of pastel brilliance;
overcast day, sundials will have to make extra efforts.

at least the next full moon will foreshadow the winter solstice
sun about to slip into my own sign, birth, yearly high-point:
hibernating with lit candles & incense makes sense
of my grand trine in fire, hearth of my heart, alight alone.

each moment has a full moon of its own.

MEMOS FROM THE PLANCHETTE OF HPB: TO WHOM IT BETTER CONCERN

MEMO 1

yes, I would like to have that
teleported
a luxurious leather-bound gold-tooled deluxe edition
of DeQuincey's Confessions of an English Opium Eater
since we got along so well in our childhood dreams:

> *"Children have a specific power of contemplating the truth,*
> *which departs as they enter the world"*

especially in the scary mirrors that lined our rooms of nightmares
(intimations of our words' worthlessness?)
glass wombs of transition
    all time,
      crossing from one juxtaposed ego
ergo, I go
  to the next
    incarnation (in-a-car-nation, USA?)

HPB I know you are inside me scratching your Nosferatu fingernails across
the slippery Parker Bros., Inc., Salem, Mass., USA ouija board
(William Fuld, are you here?) mystifying oracles whose cloudy
excruciating
  (cross, crux of matter, what's the?)

alphabets proclaim hexes, banishings, evocations that could shatter
the obelisk of this universe/solar system or some asshole's
    (imploding black holes?)

shit, HPB come out of here & make some sense
or is it I, the persona flesh-vessel you have overshadowed, fulfilled?

I think it was James Merrill who said —or if he didn't, will, should—
that the planchette of the 20th century is the electric keyboard
of the typewriter whose ouija-genie raises its ugly beauty/beast head
through these electromagnetic keys of gold, a good conductor of silver

transmuted copper: equals the center of illumination (illumined nation,
ill-mined nation) whose dollar bill contains the pyramid's crystalline
cap (eyeing what?) the sensuous kundalini in my crotch comes
from copper
— cu7—irony of the spheres: a skull & crossbones (coarse bones, corset,
coarse set?) livens my golgotha wardrobe (wordrobe): an armoire
of leering
devilish fellows: ghosts, hobgoblins, gargolyes that crouch
in the corners
of my dreams & won't let me forget the frogfilled fountain's
healing waters: when the spouts waterfall rainbow spittings

 even my prisms in the radiant southwestern window pride (parade?)
themselves in doing a good job
              palm   palimpsest
                      HPB voicings blake who?

I invoke you for the serpent power
of the five blue cobalt tears in the prayer amulet's nostril
perfumed agony encased in jewelled resonance, sarcophallic vibrations?
who is this who cries thus? is it you Koot Hoomi
of the highest mountain in the world, my heart?
                    stress?

the question is: forego form? revise?
or let stand with typos, missprints, misspelling (misshexings?)
freudian slips (dirty underwear, a word to the unwise, otherwise?)
or
  at this revision the first (2nd & 3rd)
                    cancel cancerous wordpressings:

"For that
    (the rapt one warns)
        is what papyr is meed of, made of,

hides
and hints and misses in prints"
        especially
                "Mister Typhus, Mistress Tope and all the
little typtopies"
        the keys are given
                yes yes yes
                      "aural eyeness"

the pentagram with bells (for whom tolls?) resides over my central
plex: plexus, nexus, home hearth, heart:
LANGUAGE THE TONGUE REJOICING IN ITS
HEATHENISH RELISHINGS

HPB, H.D., Mirabai, Koot Hoomi, Corelli, Bulwer-Lytton, A.A. Bailey,
Titus Rubrois aka Odin of the Deep, weird ones who enter my life
& depart
    soothsayers
        dearly departed ones
            depraved, brave, ravenous raving ones?
fable: let me amanuensis this
smith-corona electric ouija typewriter, type righter:
right the type, the archetype, set it to right, to write, our rights,
our writes
    outright!!!!!
        Blasphemously yrs,
            HPB

PS: I wouldn't mind, mind you, staying this way every day
the mindless part of it is that the power could go off any time
from an electrical thunderous storm: rain, water, flood, dreams

from the Other Side

always wanted to see how the other side lives? dies? lives of confusion
commingle with my menstrual ovulum truths, blood, uterus,
            mucus,
              pain,

                              afterbirth,
mystifying oracle.

MEMO 2

REMEMBER: nothing is ever lost
                    no not even the blood pact with the devil
JUNG or some body said
in a state

meant

that enough punishment has survived & tomorrow
not much of this will remain unerased
by the light of the silvery consciousness

the moon's full bloated
            monsoon, soon moon, monic nodes,
harmonium, harmonica

instrument of this vessel,
            empty hollow as the greek lyre (liar, man, homo-sapiens

wise man, wo-man?)

sappho
      ancient glyphic sylph, amphora-bearer, true woman
                              who loved her
SELF

PALIMPSICAL IMPRESSIONS REMAIN
ON THE ARCHETYPING MACHINE

planchette of the strange & unexpected
as planets converge & almost collide
forcing themselves on our lives
imprinting our fates with sworling whorls, worlds'

lovers conjuncting, conjugating the verb TO BE
conjunction of anti-bodies
        coitus
                mercury, salt, sulphur
                        snake, serum, truth

Hermes the healer
        bringer of NEWS
                of the cardinal directions
North, East, West, South

"It was Hermes/who took up the/
        wine jug and poured/
              wine
                      for the gods"
sapphically erotic as H.D.
                    's
                hermetic definition

I wonder if Mirabai had been Sappho in another
                            incarnation?)
(what?

HPB will you manifest me the magic ring
        semi-precious with
                carnelian & lapis
inside an eye of diamond
        Horus, hours, ours prismatic

that will permit me to understand all tongues & lick the like

of Mirabai, Sappho
        in their ancient snake-subtle tongues,
            in their original
voicings
    juicings
        rejoicings
so I open up the collected works of Patchen to

"the warm juice of suicides" by
        "all who have waited in the darkness/
are there shown in a flowering
      light"
         MOISTURE,
            salivating,
                salvation's
salty salve?

plath, sexton, berryman
      ACCIDENTS? OR
          hendrix, joplin, morrison
 doors of perception
      open up to
         paths, the lives of the poets are strewn with
suicides, really
     matricides, patricides, homocides fratricides:

WE HATE EACH OTHER WITH THE EQUAL = FORCE
OF HOW MUCH WE HATE OURSELVES
EQUATIONS OF TORMENT WRITHE FROM OUR CENTERS:
THE TREE OF GOOD & EVIL
EAT THEREOF, EAT: EAT: EAT:
              THE TIME IS RIGHT, RIPE.
HPB & you are here with me
& I feel your occult vibrations & desire the pallengenesis
of your florid corpse
       become mine
flesh, putrid alchemical dross, flaccid residue, black rose
                              ascending
incorruptible from the ashes
        red, red rose H.D. saw & pressed
to the right side of her brain
        "the reddest rose unfolds"
      or is it the left? as she thinks of red wine:

"one glass every day/ becomes an orgy" (petals unfolding,
centrifugally, in the brain)
 or is it the right? whose right is it anyway?

only wine will tell & other secretive, scorpionic forces, alchemicals
subversive
    (poets under
        stand
            sub-
                verses) to society's nerve?
lightning flashes through the ancient glass bottles presiding
on the window's ledge, ledgers of my life, my poems noted
as the years turn over & over yellowing pages, details
messages left in, out, corroded, mouse-eaten)?
where did this parenthesis begin? I never saw it
                                        (
HPB counsel me any way you can: here
I'll be your mouth:

good-bye to the
        SUN & THE MOON
                AS THE LIGHTNING STRUCK TOWER
LEANS & SPILLS ITS YODS OF ELECTRIC
                        NOUMENA INTO MY SPLIT-IN-2 SKULL:

yes   no   maybe   1234567890   what year is it anyway?)

arcane pain in the soul's eye, window
                          pane, acid rain?
I AM HPB FROM THE OTHER SIDE & I GRANT YOU THIS:

IT WAS ALL AS I PREDICTED & MORE. MUCH MORE. (YOU HAD
TO BE THERE). THERE WAS A TUNNEL. THERE WAS A LIGHT.
THERE WAS A FUNNEL OF. VIBRATING FORCES. HEAVEN &
HELL: UP/DOWN SCANNING
                REMOTE CONTROL
                    CHANNELS

I put on my whirling dervish paisley harem pants & dance this out:

scribe of the indescribable babble:
 "the process of coming unalone is terrible"
(yeah, you right, Bill, in yo' postage stamp grave, cancelled)

MY ETHERIC FORCES ARE BEING DRAINED, I AM SLIPPING AWAY:
I'LL GATHER TOGETHER MY FORCES & REGAIN THIS PARADISICAL SCARAB
INSCRIBED:

I'll just have to learn to use my muscles all over again, clearing my throat
    I'll translate:
        earthquake, hemispheres, spiders (white), volcano

bird, seated woman, palm of hand, feather, stone, the book of life, tree, 22 paths of open pain (closed, clogged, clothed in truth, beauty) fish, eye, window, mouth, vertebrae, back of head, tooth, lion, serpent, fence, sword, nail (tooth &) door, fishhook, orifice, camel, house, genitals, ox, fool, zero

etc.
    gOod-bYe, i sd I'm going

fishtail,
    you were my mother,
        thanks
 sincerely,
    sin
      seer
        eerily
          yrs,
              HPB

MEMO 3

WOMAN FINDS HER HAPPINESS IN THE ACQUISITION OF SUPERNATURAL POWERS —
    LOVE IS A VILE DREAM,
     A NIGHTMARE

these words appear in my collected writings, volume 1 — HPB

I think she overshadowed me even from the beginning
took me by the arm & led me to experience that truth:

all those garbled words thrust at Anael have gotten me nowhere
have only brought me pain, the pearl of great price
whose center is an irritable sand grain (Blake — all the world
in a grain of pain?)
                         I'll seek elsewhere,

perhaps in the streamers of etheric light that ray out
from my fingers as they shuffle the tarot images
whose rectangular forms also cast shadows from another plane

THE ANSWERS I GET COME FROM YOUR SIDE, HPB
                 CRYPTIC GYPSY
                      BORN TOO SOON

FOR THE WORLD'S MORALITY
             UNDERSTANDING
                 INTELLIGENCE
                     SOUL
                       EMBRACING

sadness, bitterness, regret are the answers I get

surely, you can do better than that?

HPB: A VALE OF TEARS! WHOEVER PROMISED YOU OTHER THAN THAT?
TRUST YOUR SENSES TO GET YOU METAPHYSICALLY BEYOND THIS BULLSHIT:
THERE ARE PATTERNS TO DREAMS EVEN DEAR JUNG NEVER DREAMED OF,
MORE TO HEAVEN & EARTH THAN EVEN ANGELS KNOW OF.
LOVE? BELOW, NO;
ABOVE, YES. YOU ARE NUMBERED WITH HEARTBEATS,

BREATHS, HAIRS, LOVES,
LIVES, MISERIES, & YES, GLORIOUS MOMENTS THAT VANISH,
                    JUST AS I
                        YRS, HPB

back at this keyboard, bored with this music? I play on
                    WORDS

alphabetic glyphs that press down hard symbols
in 2-dimensional space:

      HPB,
           send me a hologram
                    telepathic graph
of what exactly's going on over there!
                    I must know in order to understand

exactly what's going on here, will you appear in the cards, board,
planchette scribblings? will you apport me something of import (i.e.
ca$h?)

hard cash is better stash than love's hard crash! (John Donne,
where are you with your ecstasy?) is it true the venal brings us
to agape, gods' love, the gods' making? St. Francis feeding
manna to the little birds with open mouths, Giotto transfused?

HPB, are you still hungry
              on the other side? is there heartburn?
burning hearts sacrificed to the vultures of fleshly delight?

I want to move objects around the planet, I want to fly
with my astral body, I want to speak with angels, I want
to see nostradamically the past/present/future
to have access to the akashic records, new waves of supernatural song:
I belong to the invisible ones, the devil is substance, alchemical sulphur:
suffer in matter, the cross:
                  how much more
shit
do I have to take

do I have to prove
what is there left
to write about

except dreams?
 HPB: WHEN I WAS IN CONSTANTINOPLE MY FAITHFUL DOG
RALPH RAN OFF & COULDN'T FIND HIM FOR DAYS. I
CONSULTED A DERVISH ORACLE WHO SWIRLED & SWORE
HE DISAPPEARED INTO THE LUMINOUS CIRCLE
OF A MAGIC MOON: THE GROTESQUE DWARFWOMAN
DREW AROUND HER A CHALK CIRCLE & FILLED IT WITH
QUAINT SIGNS & HEXES, THEN SHE WAS WHIRLED BY HER
ANKLES & TOLD ME EXACTLY WHERE TO FIND HIM.
I FOUND HIM. DOES THAT ANSWER YOUR QUESTION?

I HOPE SO. DON'T IN THE FUTURE BOTHER ME WITH SUCH
TRIFLES.

YRS, HPB

the kundalini serpent moves its phallic fire up my spine
& you are mine, astral body. to hell with those vile dreams

MEMO 4

anima mundi encapsuled in crystal
of rock salt, prismatic snapshots
of flux, my face dissembling into the earth

's bowels, emerging from the mountain
's pond, the waterfall rainbowed naked
around the luminous egg like a snake
& my body cracks out of the splinters
covered with sublimated water droplets:

HPB reaching through me onto this plane
of jewelled mandala boxes with 7 semi-

precious stones, one glowing with prophecy
one swirling into green-blue depths,
red/blue/yellow/green peacocks (or winged
scarabaeus, dung to sun?) enamelled outspread wings:
fish, star, bird, beetle, moon brought
into true relief by brass/copper marriage:
box of my dreams what you contain is nothing
yet everything I know or have ever known
is within you. Oriental & Egyptian
alchemical glyph & Jung's western mysticism
contained within the glass pentagram:
one a real prismatic crystal, one just glass
containing another spherical multi-faceted
crystal: within, within, within

reaching deeper, deeper, ever deeper into me,
HPB please make my fingers on these electric keys
be your 20th century planchette, moving aphabetically
sympathetically across these encounters with the

DARK SHADOW of self within self within, THE BOX.

just now I have to stop & make sure my plants
are still green & that windows let in blue/gray light
that my wood floors are brown, oak table & chairs still oaken,
no lost molecules flying off into black holes

of SELF

there is a mailbox right outside the front door
with nothing in it

what news? prima materia of all hope & despair.
messages of the ages, hints, out-&-out charlatan lies,
boring obligations to society, words to the wise & words
to bring salt to eyes:

threading through needle of: HPB's ISIS UNVEILED:
unavailed, unreviled:

this time I draw the mandala'd curtain
across the front window just to box
myself off a little more
in this cornered moment, cornucopia
of my sensual hungers, abandoning the dark self

to light: HPB, I'm yr box
come to me at this very instant when my prismed
lamp lurches with snakes above this planchette type-
writing machine.
        even my fingernails are painted
silvery glacier blue for the occasion,
special conductors of your mantic vibrations:

HPB: YOU'VE LOCKED ME INTO CAPITALS NOW
& NOTHING I SAY CAN ESCAPE YOU, QUICKSILVER
TRICKSTER AT THE MERCURIAL FOUNTAIN
WHERE 7 SIMULTANEOUS PROCESSES SYNCHRONIZE
TO FORM THESE VERY WORDS: ANAEL STILL
WATCHES YOU OVER THE GLITTERY DISPLAY OF
YOUR ORDINARY OBJECTS IMBUED WITH GLAMOUR, SYMBOLS:
RHINESTONES THAT CONVEY THE SOUL'S LIGHT
TO MY SHADOW
COMBINING WITH YOURS: YOU ARE NANCY, BUT I AM HPB
WRITING THROUGH YOUR RING-LADEN FINGERS:
I HAVE MASTERS WHO GUIDE ME
& A RAINBOW FROM THE PRISM LAMP ABOVE ME
FALLS UPON EVERY WORD YOU ARE TYPING NOW:
THAT WAS NO COINCIDENCE!
        I AM AFRAID TO TAKE YOU OVER
FOR TOO LONG PERIODS, OR YOU MAY NEVER COME BACK
 TO YOURSELF.
        TEMPORARILY WANING,
            YRS, HPB

HPB you scare me sometimes with your secret doctrines:
I look at your profiled gypsy portraits (yes photographs
or your corporeal vibrations) but the one I'm searching

for right now in mist must stare you directly in your mystical eyes:
I cry when I find the photo & realize that I gaze
into my own eyes: yours: mine: you are my spirit
my grandmother, with your russian gypsy tarot, buddhist,
theosophist (yes, you even remind me of my christian scientist
grandmother who now visits me in dreams from your realm)
we've all melted into each other, undifferentiated woman
in cross-sections of time who sought & seek light & love
wrestling with the question:

is it to be found in physical male/female union
or in the rich dark boxed-in caverns of our bivalved
anima/animus minds?

HPB, you keep whispering to me that love is a "vile nightmare"
or your original French
        "vilain rêve, un cauchemar"
et, dans le français, vous savez, the words mêre, mer
are homophonous with mother, ocean

so "nightmares" freudian horses, dark ocean depths,
fear of the primordial mother-womb
I think it's all of the above

& more.

PS
I am afraid of you, but I think you were afraid
in your time

of certain things

in my time
I'm coming to grips with, in this strange drug-induced
20th century schizophrenia, split-in-2-skull?

lightning struck tower
bringing destruction of the past
with enlightenment to follow

even with hostility of chtonic forces
aleister crowley's satanic trump:

something keeps me coming out ahead
of time? in time?

PPS

walking without shoes in the moist green
grass preserves my illusion of sanity,
ephemeral beast fuming in the dragon's glass stomach:

the serpent, candleflame, square, triangle, circle:
the kundalini spirit, I see all these
in helen's rippling poet painting that says:
woman can synthesize (yes, try on sin for size,
sighs, our glamorous guises, disguises) all four
anti-bodies & create new forms:

anima/animus, physical/metaphysical, sex/love

ALL WITHIN HERSELF

& while she knows that a whole man is hard to find

SHE JUST WANTS COMPLETION WITH ANOTHER
WHO DOESN'T NEED HER, JUST DESIRES HER COMPLETE.

HPB, I think you were frustrated there in the 19th century
& kept searching your crystal balls, planchettes
table rappings, yes spiritual questing hoping to believe
that love is a vile dream "un cauchemar"

but if it weren't so, why have you come back to haunt me
to overshadow, outrageous icon of fin de siècle hysteria?

WHAT CAN YOU TELL ME? WHAT CAN I SHOW YOU?

let's be separate in our real spheres

of ominous truths

let's be demon lovers to our shadow selves
& maybe we'll both wake up from our centuries' vile dreams
& enter the millennium

    whole as creators
      whole creatures
        animal selves

I AM RAPT WITH ATTENTION, RAPPING IN YOUR WALLS
I CAN SPELL YOU A NEW MEMORY BANK ACROSS MY SLIPPERY PLANCHETTE
CODED WITH CRESCENT MOON LIGHT, COUNTERFEIT SALT-ENCRUSTED DROPLETS
  WASH OVER MY SUBLIME FACE, CONDENSATION
      OVERLAPPING CONVERSATIONS

YRS IN NIGHTMARES' SCREECHING FINGERNAILS
    ACROSS THE PLANCHETTE'S PLAINS,
  (THE MASTERS HAVE COMMANDED ME TO LEAVE)
DEMATERIALISING YOUR SPIRITUAL SISTER —
     YES NO MAYBE, HPB

BEAR DREAMS

These poems/dreams were written over a period of time from the mid 90's up to the present. The dreams began earlier but I could not write about them until an encounter with David Carson, co-creator of *The Medicine Cards*, followed by the synchronicity of stumbling across James Hillman's book, *Dream Animals*.

THE CARE & FEEDING OF ANIMAL IMAGES

> "I became more and more concerned with the animals rather than with the dreamers. I had departed from both scientific empirical research and practical therapy in favor of conservationism — a phenomenological care of animal images, resisting their becoming translated into data on the one hand and personal meaning on the other."
> - James Hillman, *Dream Animals*

i

the whitened bears, mildewed, askewed
were stacked up around the walls
like Mayan images at a temple site—
decapitated skulls from a ritual ballgame—
only we were in the water, a circular stream
where I encountered sea tortoises swimming beneath me
intricate runes or tattoos etching the shells' scrimshaws
wavering into the depths:

near the bears holding their cubs were
large cats, panthers, jaguars? with dogs
in their jaws, clenched by the neck, not killing them
just transporting them

the stream lurched into stone walls
guarding the way out into the gulf beyond, where
my friend had made it through in her speed boat
but I was motorless, paddling my way
through churning waters, having to turn around,
not daring to cross paths with the large cats

somehow the thought gestates ...
all this has something to do with the walls
of my uterus, but I let go of the image
let it float out to the delta

when I return to the party on the houseboat
someone hands me a tropical drink

in a skull

bone-colored bears fasten themselves
onto the walls of my dream

ii

the black or dark brown bears
began appearing in my dreams years ago
shocking me with their presence
I had never concerned my waking brain
with bears at all, no, gorillas were my obsession
my lesson, my Jungian archetype

the first appeared in my old shotgun single
on Leonidas Street, where I was perched on top
of an armoire with antique mirrors
whose depths were mysteries, histories
of dreamtime & dreamspace

I was terrified the bear wanted to snatch away
my civilization, why was it in my house?
And why was it after me and why was I afraid
for my domestic dogs and cats
who I wanted to protect from this wild
invasive rape
of my privacy, my subconscious
my ego wanting to interpret even in the dream
the Jungian opposites, nature vs. society

the dark bear was reaching for me
with magnified nightmare claws as I jumped
from one high piece of wood furniture to the next
predatory adrenaline clutching my throat with silent screams,
but I was never really scared, just puzzled

iii

bear dreams repeated themselves in varying

themes, always with the same elements
over-and-over, year-after-year
until finally I became conscious of actually having
the dreams. Always trying to escape the data
the symbols and the dream dictionary's
anthropomorphic *personal meanings.*

then one dream was different: a large
looming, luminous white bear stood on its hind legs
watching me and making no judgments
filling me with awe & reverence
he was not in my house
he was much larger than that and I knew
his whiteness was significant
but I was unable to decipher the message
if there was one it was blurred in the snow of
phenomenology.

iv

when I moved to my new house that
I own, not rent, around the corner
my first bear dream happened like this:
a bear cub had escaped from the Audubon Zoo
and it was at my back door, my dogs and cats
got out of the way, they were safe and I felt
compassion for the small, helpless cub
thinking I needed to return it to the zoo
feeling as though it would resolve something.

when my friend called from the Cosmic Crystal
saying that one of the authors of *The Medicine Cards*
was in town, did I want a reading, I leapt at the chance.
he also needed a large space for a medicine wheel ceremony.
I offered my still empty attic bedroom space.

during the reading I could not *creatively visualize*
my totem animal on cue, and frustrated, I said look,
I can't do this but let me tell you about my bear dreams.

when I got to the part about the bear cub
David Carson looked appalled and yelled, "NO!!!"
you can't send it back to the zoo
don't you understand, the bear has been inviting you
to become its ally, to join its bearhood.
If it goes back to the zoo you are doomed—
it will shrink and disappear—
you have to invite it back to you
as a full-grown bear essence
large and fearsome.
so much for Jungian archetypes I thought
this is for real.

the shamanic drums from the medicine wheel
still beat in my head, the vibrations haunt the
attic, the bears dance and float
down through
stars and galaxies through the double-terminated
crystal in the center
of my dream catcher.

v

the next dreams came all at once
—I think there were three—
but they're confused:
I was at a lodge in the mountains, staring out
a big panoramic window at several bears who beckoned
for me to go to them, for me to let them in and I did.

then I was out on the ice where a dark brown bear
cut a circular hole and I thought we would fish.
but then I was Bear, I was in Bear & yet outside Bear
in the dreamtime of no vanishing points:
Bear's face began to flow into multiple images of
humans—all the races and sexes throughout the history of earth
commingled and swirled, changing into each other
in a hallucinogenic, geometric pattern
and suddenly I knew that Bear

was the grandmother and grandfather of all animals—
humans included.

after that Bear didn't visit my dreams for awhile
and when Bear did I still kept my distance
honoring the presence, thankful.

recently Bear revealed a humorous nature:
Bear was watching me with fascination and amusement—
I was interesting to Bear! I felt nurtured—we were mirrors.
Bear and I are not yet finished with each other.

We feed off each other's images.

WHAT BEAR WANTS

> "Anything that comes at you in a dream wants you, has an intention
> that may not be the intention you as a dreamer attribute to it.
> Do we know what the bear wants?"
> - James Hillman, *Dream Animals*

food, shelter, dreams.
dreams of food, caves of love
contact with aliens,
a search for something in common

with the tourists in their shiny transports
housing food, snacks, potato chips,
peanut butter, chocolate chip cookies.
breaking into jeeps, vans, tents
that magically appear in their territory—
national parks are for people, not bears.

some human gets mauled
some bears are "put down" by park rangers:
"They became too dependent on junk food
instead of their natural pantry of beehives &
salmon—too much trouble in
these microwave times. Instant dinner."

what did the black bear from Florida
want in Baton Rouge backyards
foraging through garbage cans, scaring the
shit out of suburban housewives?
the bear escaped from the preserve
over and over, wanting to roam Louisiana
where naturalists scratched their heads
with dumb amazement.

what dreams does Bear feast on
lumbering through images
hibernating in high-tech caves:

are we in Bear's dreams
& what do we want from Bear?

what draws us closer
at the end of the millennium—
civilization encroaching on nature—
or does Bear just want a condo at the beach
with wetbar and proximity to malls?

what did Bear see on the other side of the mountain—
you, me in our dreams of pure serenity
inside our iron security & alarm systems—
safe from wild stalking dream-forms

does Bear know what I want?

I want Bear to drag me down
into a wet, jagged cave
dark as a sardine can
swallow me whole for dinner & dream
my dismembered torso back into the stars.

I want Bear to ravage me
& spit me out syllable by syllable
cell by cell until I am holy
until Bear pelts me with blessings.

what Bear wants is Bear's business.

WHITE SPIRIT BEAR VANISHING

this bear is not a symbol
neither is its vanishing *(banishing)*
that's the point

vanishing that is
into the edge of the painting
folded down like a sheet
the sides of the canvas
stapled to the wood frame

framed into vanishing *(banishing)*
by greed & profit

a hole punched through the canvas

white spirit bear pushed to the edge
of the canadian island
every fourth black bear
born is white
a genetic miracle
brown-eyed, not albino
not a freak, a gift

clearcutting the northern rainforest
for trees, for paper to print this poem
the bear leaps out at you
its whiteness freezing you
its fleeting omnipresence
paralyzing you
whitewashing the empty canvas

in my dream it was white
the bear vanishing into the white
staining the world, stunning

a rainbow of white arching

over this gray vista
hologram just visible
from certain angles
holy light filtered by spectrums
I see stretching forever across this page.

white spirit bear concerns me
converging & crashing in the forest
with no one to hear

white spirit bear wants me
I know this as it crosses the tundras
of my peripheral vision

white spirit bear
stalks the corners
of my REM cycles

where the dream is not a symbol
it's a long-distance call

from the rim
of the compass

vanishing *(banishing)*
the bear points home

BEAR FLOATS IN MY CEREBRAL CORTEX

Bear attacks campers in Colorado
first time in thirty years
rips tents, limbs who knows why
rips my dreams in two
tearing fabrics
of telltale hearts' forensic fibs

Bear slits my throat
with wretched hope
writhes sinuously throughout
my vascular system of veins & vines
o tarzan who greased the ...
apocalyptical jackals grope through
the crags & crannies of my brain's
rippling riptides and rigid mountains
forests slipping down slopes

nothing of this is even a sliver of intent that
last nights' insomnia told me to write
it was so spirited & metaphysical
an advent an adventure
an ending to this well-wrought urn
earn, earnest the importance of ...

I never found Bear hibernates en hiver,
lost words on a couch of demolished comfort

bear somersaulting in my blood corpuscles
DNA structure
bear startling stars and structural
format in my veins listening to silent white light
squatting with piss in the snow ... where art thou now

haunted hunted one ... in the midst of Leo, dog days & nights
inside a twelve-sided pentagonal crystal
caving in.

BEAR HIBERNATES EN HIVER

& dreams a new dance for a new season
that leaves winter out
of the picture
in the cold
a solstice of despair turning
incrementally into an equinox
of fractal omens, idylls of buds
bursting, breathing fresh fire

Bear looks forward to skipping a whole season
hated outwardly/ hoarded inwardly the jewels
of isolation glowing with spasmodic
diastole/systole jerks of sympathetic nerves'
arrhythmic snores
diving down deeper into the dream
into the stores of fleshfood
nourishing the levels
of knowledge
of events
past & future.

seer shaman for the tribe
nearing its endtime
everything falls apart when it must
when its spiral winds down
when winter finishes its big sleep

Bear dreams the dreams the whole tribe
will paint & write about
in the next millennium
so Bear dreams big dreams, wild & vivid dreams
rainbow dreams with fine new colors undreamt
for millenniums.
Bear shakes his/her head in his/her dream
& snorts with delight
at the new scents that will unfold in the spring

newness never seen, touched, heard, tasted
before in the universe, the Pleiades & beyond
any stars man could have found with telescopes

Bear dances in his/her sleep
the dance of new beginnings
legs twitching with elegance
proportion & glamour
waiting for the sun to pour
out its radiant streamers
kneading the earth
to feed the multitudes heart-grains
& other necessary images.

BEAR AT THE BACK DOOR

standing dark in the dream the back yard
in uptown New Orleans
you couldn't really be there outrageous beast
of another world—but I'm dreaming this
and I'm supposed to know that I'm dreaming
I'm not supposed to be scared and running
back into the safety of the house—I'm supposed
to invite you in—I'm supposed to let you bite
my right shoulder between my neck and ear.

I'm having another Bear Dream I shout in the dream
with conscious unconsciousness or whatever reality I'm in
so I rush back to the fence and wait for the Bear to bite
then I'm awake in whatever reality I live in
I think I'm supposed to write this poem because the bite
was on my right—gateway to the left brain of
creative energy—so I'm writing this
just because I was bit by the bear in my dream.
I search for twigs and berries
I bury the dream in convoluted synapses
& let the dogs out.

BEAR COMES HOME TO DINE ON YOUR EAR

what's this I hear? Bear grumbles
taking whatever time is needed to rethink
the last winter dream white snow black cave ink
what could possibly happen

between now and then plus some
weird egos with indigestion
churning the hard drives intestines
with druids and fluids, enzymes
in between times reflux
of stars bowel movements in the sky

I didn't eat a thing all season
may be the reason for all this churning
but I can't compare my cave to Plato's
abdomen, domain, no reason to complain

and yet still didn't lose weight just gained
compassion or was it passion for your wand
your word, your smile. I listen to your music
and dance the bear dance, the barely there dance
of your chaste skeleton, your ghostly pirouettes.

your brother did live in my house once
before everything got weird, before deaths.
what breaths. what season. no reason.

BEAR DREAMS Y2K

white dreams filter the images
nudges from another realm
Bear snores & remembers REM sites
restores hordes of foodstuffs
nourishing the brain's cache of
time-travel: the new millennium
slips by unnoticed in hibernation
white house white nation
wintery nation of discontent
Bear rolls over on the other side
of alpha states:

the forest of molecular structure forms trees
& in the center a canopy bed of crystals radiates
an old woman lying on its jagged mattress
dreaming incandescent rivers & streams:

Bear wants to grab all of it & run
with illicit rainbows of booty.
Bear has moments of moral quandary:
if I take it will I be punished?
I want it. I want it now. Bear grabs
a huge chunk of crystal, breaks it off
the mother lode, rushes to the edge
of the forest & snorts: an old woman laughs.

Bear you Fool she shouts, you can have
anything you want, take it—it's yours
for the taking. guilt is deleted from Bear's brain.

when Bear wakes up, Bear holds a huge
crystal cluster brimming with sunlight
ancient lineages of interstellar DNA, heritage.

rage Bear rage against the law enforcement

of the light: now it seems the edges of dreams
permeate what Bear desires—new evenings
with new sunsets curtailing the news:

find the source—informed or otherwise—
finite possibilities forge geometric vortices
voicings & rambling grunts: the crystal balanced
& buried at the window of peace paces
urgently, gently, across the record keeper's dreams:
prayers through pentagrams of sliding light
surge & tides push up forgotten garbage & treasures
to the foremost lobe of the milleniums' new brain.
Bear turns invisible in the helix of frosty magnification.
Y2K, just a joke on late-night talk-shows. Double-terminated.

& another thousand years
eclipse the mounds of buried crystals
on an island in Nova Scotia—the salmon
are rushing through pure alpha waves
in Bear's hungry brain: Y2K swallowed
in a moment of grace—disappearing.

next morning the newspaper
is lying on the front porch just
like yesterday. Same sun, planets
circling the mysteries.
Bear yawns & stretches, eyes clear.

BEAR MARKET

this millennium another Louisiana black bear
lumbers across the parishes puzzled, lost
or just renegade? The preservation a filmy dream
of swirling visions/prisms, recently prosperous ponderings
now plunging precariously close to extinction
profits flatlining head, heart
the rangers say he's confused, not dangerous
treat him like your pet dog if you see
his dream-image romping in your backyard.

if you haven't foreclosed
brought your dogs and cats to a shelter
live in your SUV until it's repossessed
then you can go find a cave
cash in your 401K, sleep deep in winter
your discontent, don't worry Prospero
will save you when Bear wakes

the earth quakes, shuddering fire and smoke
mirrors signal, play tricks with tsunamis and typhoons
Sedna aligns with Mars
whales maligned, captured and enslaved
for public entertainment, holding the earth's
light grids intact, even as they are slaughtered
by those they want to save: us humans
who dream they are bears foraging through forests
of greed – victims of crashes & fluctuations
emotional kneejerks

just let a black bear into your heart
feed on it frenzied with hunger
the dream inserts intself into your spleen
spit out the gnawing images, cartilage
knuckles of butchered civilization

Bear has riches undreamed of

stashed away in his cave, hoarded
for the winter solstice when time ends
stalactic teeth, crystal skulls, mayan codes
taking stock of cancelled history.

BEAR EATS THE MAYAN CALENDAR & AN OYSTER PO-BOY

> "Traps baited with peanut butter have not snared the black bear that has been prowling Bayou Dularge at night, rifling through the garbage. So residents are now trying tastier grub, such as Cajun cooking ... succulent po-boys and seafood."
> — Associated Press (in *The Times-Picayune*, Sept. 16, 2009)

1.

Bear reaches into the dark void and withdraws an oyster po-boy,
dressed – creole tomatoes, lettuce, mayo, lots of hot sauce
plus a galaxy of crispy fried oysters
sizzling like stars in the inky night sky —
a cauldron in the Pleiades or is it Ursa Minor?
the big dipper in the garbage of the suburbs –
even the creole gumbo is toxic
the red beans & arsenic famous louisiana rice
sucking up poisons in the water
environmental chemicals create arsenic and old rice:
mix in a soupcon of BP oil spill — et voila!
species are disappearing – black bears, fish
wetlands, pelicans —
and god forbid the oysters, shrimp and crawdads.

Bear knows this and is grabbing his/her last meal before extinction.

it's 2012 on the mayan calendar: ahau: light: time is extinct
executed in a timely fashion: the dodecahedron crystal, 13th gate:
bear holds it up to his/her eye magnifying the sun:
all 12 sides are pentagrams
with rainbow inclusions in the cubed center, galactic center,
black hole:

polar bears melt, the poles shift.

white spirit bears are caught in crystalline stasis:

a Louisiana black bear is found shot in the red river
wildlife preserve —
transmitter collar useless. time stops.
Bear stops and spots an etouffee, blackened salmon
blackened moon at the autumnal equinox: pearls emit from oysters.

the candidates debate. continents collide.
religions inflame. governments collapse.
Bear ambles on confounded and curious, hungry & adept.
when the student is ready …
the planet implodes … unless.

2.

13th crystal skull completes the grid:
Bear grins and waves at residents
who think they own the territory, a theory Bear rejects.
humans don't own the planet, fruits of the land & sea:
Bear satiates.

fibonacci counts the sequence of spirals, fingerprints, seashells,
DNA double helixes, golden ratios, sacred geometry, platonic solids,
crystals, bears & animal fetishes:
not rational, not left-brained, a no-brainer:
Bear doesn't bother with such musings,
just wants food: will forage for food:
Bear in Colorado raids candy store.

Bear's brothers & sisters uprise:
coyotes attack joggers, raccoon attacks old woman
cougar mangles hiker, dolphin attacks swimmer,
whale attacks trainer:
the animals are uprising, surprising: quantum leaps:
north Africans, Middle Easterners attacking
their leaders, downtrodden for centuries,
their women uprising, surprising …

Bear heads to another backyard, another state.

Bear attacks an oyster po-boy – not on his food pyramid.
Bear attacks the Mayan code, eats hieroglyphs …
dances a trecena in 13 steps
hiccups & burps civilizations' fractal menus.

Bear looks up to the night sky,
waits for the winter solstice
pines for a po-boy dressed with prisms.

Bear's heart explodes into a hurricane
of hungry dreams.

BEAR DREAMS THE HUNTER'S MOON HANGS IN THE ATTIC

like a bat in a cave glittering with
rutilated crystals: I wake in the middle
of the full October moon
weeks away from the winter solstice
in the year twenty-twelve:
Bear doesn't want me to
stop dreaming or Bear will die into the light
jump off the canvas painted by humans:

Bear will dive into the black hole of galactic center
the moment time ends in the dark rift
of the Milky Way, finger of God
pointing to the sacred tree, cosmic cross:
I see Bear looking down at me from a jagged hole
in my attic patiently waiting for a sign
that the calendar will mark a new day
a paradigm for human hearts to sing to the planet:

Bear is changing form, transmuting
into a BearWolf at the full moon's
gravitational pull—
eating the carcass dripping with blood
predator of dreams, digesting images
collector of prisms, chomping down
huge chunks of light:

on the threshold of all hallow's eve,
all saints & all souls' days of sorrows,
les très riches heures, books of hours:

I thought my dreams of Bear were done
but Bear won't let me be: I bow down & ask
forgiveness—ask to be Bear's host
at the communion, to mingle with Bear
to slide down esophagus, my exoskeleton

swallowed & crunched like potato chips
in the tourist parks—pommes de terre
poèmes de terror, territorial rites
of passage:

Bear hunts time:
Bear eats time:
Bear bides his/her time:

Bear waits to tear me apart
to gorge on my heart
to bring me to light:

can I live without Bear's dream?

BEAR DREAMS CRYSTAL SKULLS
AT THE WINTER SOLSTICE

I am chased by Bear on a bicycle
holding a crystal skull on a stick –
I am on a bicycle with a crystal skull
being chased by a bear on a bicycle
holding a crystal skull
pedaling on Carrollton streets towards my house
which is at the corner of Hunab Ku
& the Galactic Womb—black hole,
sun behind the sun—umbilical cord of the planet
my uterus filled with stars, asteroid goddesses
lightyears, giving birth to stargate 12:12:12:

Bear wants to go to the Oak Street Poboy fest
craving the barbecue shrimp & pecan encrusted
trout meunière: my house is a hospital
with winding hallways, spiraling nebulas
& I visit a sick friend, sick mother, dead father:

Bear waits for 12:21:12, numbed by numbers
painted onto a canvas stretched to quantum dimensions
holograms at the edge of galactic butterfly's
emergence from hellhole
21st century cocoon of lies,
wars, pillaging & sacking mother earth's womb,
illegitimate rape: mountains, rivers, lakes, seas, blue skies:
as Venus, Mercury & Saturn align over the pyramid at Giza
dolphin murderers stalk the gulf coast, mutilating truth:
two more Louisiana black bears found shot
on protective preserves, terror on land & sea:

Bear devours a poboy dressed with 13 crystal skulls:
what Bear sees on the other side of the mountain
may not be another mountain: poles shift &
continents drift: Bear wakes up from dark dreams

& watches the sun rise, hungry as usual
dumpster diving into civilizations' refusals:

watch Bear dance: watch Bear lumber
into the vanishing point, into the skulls' lambent
directions: magnetic North-East-West-South
deranged by melting ice caps:

Bear hibernates in a womb-cave dreaming of butterflies
of spring of salmon splashing through rushing streams
of light emitting piezo-electric sparks
from homo-sapient numbskulls:

Bear delights, eats light: 12:21:12:
numbers gyrate as the world winds down

Bear sleeps & dreams of spring:
13 skulls sing & smile at death
millenniums heave, volcanoes erupt

uncorrupt, Bear lumbers off the canvas:

Made in the USA
Charleston, SC
09 October 2015